No Job? No Prob!

How to Pay Your Bills, Feed Your Mind,

and Have a Blast When You're Out of Work

Nicholas Nigro

Skyhorse Publishing

For Nicholas Nigro Sr., who appreciated life's simple things: reading books, watching the Yankees, and growing tomatoes.

Skyhorse Publishing books may be purchased in bulk at special discounts for sales promotion, corporate gifts, fund-raising, or educational purposes. Special editions can also be created to specifications. For details, contact the Special Sales Department, Skyhorse Publishing, 555 Eighth Avenue, Suite 903, New York, NY 10018 or info@skyhorsepublishing.com

www.skyhorsepublishing.com

10 9 8 7 6 5 4 3 2 1

Library of Congress Cataloging-in-Publication Data
Nigro, Nicholas J.
No job? No prob! : how to pay your bills, feed your mind, and have a blast when you're out of work / Nicholas Nigro.
p. cm.
ISBN 978-1-60239-350-9 (alk. paper)
1. Unemployed—United States. 2. Unemployed—United States—Finance, Personal. 3. Insurance, Unemployment—United States. 4. Job hunting—United States. 5. Unemployment—United States. I. Title.
HD5724.N54 2008
332.0240086'9410973--dc22
2008016721

Printed in China

CONELY BRANCH

Contents

Part Three

KICKING BACK

Part Four

FEELING GOOD

ACKNOWLEDGMENTS

Foremost, I wish to thank my agent, June Clark, who originally thought of me for this undertaking and made it a reality. I would also like to thank my editor, Alaina Sudeith, who nurtured an intriguing concept into a full-length book, as well as the many capable hands who edited this manuscript at Skyhorse. For all of you who offered ideas and suggestions along the way, consider yourself duly thanked. Finally, to the fraternity of jobless men and women who turned unemployment lemons into lemonade, your powers of example were the wind beneath the wings of this book.

Unemployed and Proud

For myself, I am an optimist.
It does not seem to be much use being anything else.
—Winston Churchill

History is awash with men and women who—either voluntarily or involuntarily—found themselves without a job and source of income, but who subsequently righted their seemingly sinking ships and sailed on to bigger, better, and brighter horizons. This is precisely the forward-moving current you want to get swept up in.

However, be ever-vigilant, jobless traveler! Watch out for those riptides. If you equate your unemployment days and nights with a devastating shipwreck, you more than likely will emerge from the ordeal bruised and battered. It's a self-fulfilling prophecy that you would be wise to avoid at all costs.

If, on the other hand, you regard your joblessness as a mere life pothole—albeit one that may shake, rattle, and roll you for a moment or two—you'll find yourself in the enviable position of total control of your situation. Strive always to be the lord and master of your own destiny. Never for a moment relinquish stewardship of your today, your tomorrow, and the tomorrow after that.

Every Ending Is a New Beginning

Positive thinking at this stage in your life and times is critical to both your present straits and your future prospects. No one can dispute that the absence of a job and a corresponding income stream is a potentially alarming scenario. But if you firmly believe that your current jobless-ness is merely a temporary glitch in your abiding life expedition, your outlook will noticeably brighten, as will your chances for entering into a new and improved job, career, or business startup.

Most of us know people who lost their jobs and immediately pushed the panic button. But, more often than not, these same men and women recovered with what, in many instances, could be described as genuine aplomb. In other words, they unearthed new jobs, careers, or business enterprises that—*courtesy of having been an unemployment statistic*—proved most fortuitous for both their short- and long-term futures.

Count Your Blessings-in-Disguise

The oft-repeated idiom, "It's a blessing in disguise," rings true time and again for countless unemployed folks who find themselves a bit down at first, but who endure and live to tell about the dazzling light show they encounter at the ends of their jobless tunnels—metaphorically speaking, of course. Rising from the jobless ashes like a phoenix is a recurring theme for many transitory retirees—aka the unemployed. And this isn't to suggest that because you're out of work, you are somehow the stuff of legend, akin to baseball icon Lou Gehrig, "the luckiest man on the face of the earth." Gehrig, after all, was terminally ill—a dying man—when he uttered those immortal words. You aren't on the way out; *you're on the way up.* No death certificate has yet listed the cause of death as unemployment. It is therefore prudent that you treat this work-free snapshot in your life as both an ending *and a beginning,* because that's exactly what it is.

Unemployment Transformations Happen Every Day to Everyday People Like You

What follows is an illuminating case in point from the reality laboratory that vividly illustrates the *endings as beginnings* philosophy as it specifically applies to surviving the vicissitudes of joblessness and, more importantly, emerging whole from its sometimes smothering and rather extended shadow. You are sure to appreciate the protagonist's accomplishments and how persons in your situation replicate them every single day.

So, let us turn the clock back to 1972, when a young man by the name of Rich Covello receives his diploma—a bachelor of science in business administration, specializing in management—from Manhattan College in the tony Riverdale section of the Bronx. Upon graduation, Rich's fledgling jobs in the corporate milieu find him—yes—donning a suit and tie, but essentially toiling in glorified drudgework with less than stellar compensation for his consistently conscientious labors. Rich manages the electronics department in the most internationally renowned department store in the world—Macy's at Herald Square. He subsequently assumes comparable job positions in now defunct department stores such as A&S, Kresge's, and Britt's. Throughout Rich's early years in the labor force, which take him through the colorful decade of the 1970s, he collects unemployment benefits on multiple occasions.

During these aforementioned stretches of joblessness, Rich, to employ his choice of words, "schemes." This may ring pejorative to untrained ears, and maybe even a little nefarious, but scheming is Rich's personally preferred phrase for *brainstorming*, which is always a prized card in your jobless hand—an ace up your sleeve. In other words, Rich utilizes snippets of his jobless free time to, in essence, divine his future. He simultaneously goes back to school to earn his MBA degree. Importantly, Rich also takes full advantage of his unemployment freedom to have a fair share of good times. A big baseball fan, he visits ballparks in cities ranging from Pittsburgh's now obsolete Three Rivers Stadium to Chicago's historic Wrigley Field. In between bouts of traveling, he inaugurates Monopoly and Clue board game tournaments with his friends and neighbors.

As fate would have it, Rich's final jobless stint—which he doesn't realize at the time is his last ride into the unemployment sunset—comes attached to a veritable pot of gold. (And no, it has nothing to do with any kind of generous severance package.) Rather, tired of toiling for others in the corporate rough-and-tumble, Rich opts to go into business for himself. The only questions that remain are: What kind of business should it be? What kind of business *will* it be?

Rich's unemployment-inspired quality time enables him to feel, among many things, a health and wellness tsunami stirring beneath the surface of the consumer consciousness. He briefly considers opening up a restaurant that sells salads *and salads alone*. He researches all of the minutiae that such an undertaking would entail, and even has potential business names at the ready: Salad King and Land of a Thousand Salads top the lengthy list. Eventually, the logistics of a venture of this width and breadth prove too problematic for him at his relatively young age and limited resources. Salad King would necessitate some serious venture capital and a few ready, willing, and able risk-takers to invest in a wholly unique kind of eatery for a different day. Remember: this is the late 1970s. And suffice it to say that lenders brandishing sacks full of money to breathe life into this trailblazing idea, including family and friends, are hard to come by.

To make a long story short, Rich speaks with a neighbor of his who owns and operates a small pet food and supply shop on Manhattan's Upper East Side. This entrepreneur fervently believes that the pet care trade is an up-and-coming sector of commerce, even though most people regard it as a grubby way to earn a buck. He importunes Rich to get in on its ground floor before it's too late.

And so, with a younger partner to help pay the bills and fulfill the workload, Rich makes the quantum leap and purchases a mom-and-pop shop that sells cat and dog merchandise. It is located on a busy boulevard in the New York City borough of Queens and called Pet Nosh. This modest acquisition of an existing store with an established cash flow enables Rich to subsist—although quite meagerly at first—while building up the business. His mother nevertheless refers to his entrepreneurial adventure as a "hobby," and anticipates that her son will soon come to his senses and return to the *cornucopia of benefits* and *lifetime of security* that America's corporate world bestows upon its employees.

Fast-forward seventeen years to 1996: Rich and his two business partners sell their eight pet food and supply superstores to retail chain Petco for $19.1 million. Fast forward five more years to 2001: Rich is back in the very same business for another go around, and is today successfully competing against the Goliath retailer who bought him out lock, stock, and barrel, as well as with the industry leader, PetSmart. His new superstores are called Pet Goods (PetGoods.com).

The abiding lesson to be gleaned from this rags-to-riches story is that Rich transformed job loss (in his particular case, multiple job losses) into a career and business that has made him a few dollars along the way. He also had oodles of fun orchestrating his next moves. And this isn't to intimate that his course is right for you, or even remotely practical for your particular life circumstances and interests. It's meant only to exemplify what you need to do while traversing the unemployment bridge. That is, take an inventory of who you are right now and ask yourself what you would like to happen in both your immediate and long-term futures. You've got to visualize what you want your new beginning—post-unemployment—to resemble. It's your call. You've experienced an unmistakable ending (the loss of a job), and now it's time to assess where you can go from here—where, in fact, you want to go from this point onward.

Unemployment Benefit #1

You are no longer in earshot of a "Mexican Hat Dance" cell phone ringtone all day, every day.

EXERCISE

Endings as Beginnings: Jobless Test Number One

Ask yourself and honestly answer these questions to acquire a genuine feel for the impending course you want to chart:

1. Do you want to remain in the same job field that you were previously in? _____

2. If you answered "yes" to #1, which of the following best describes your reason for wanting to remain in the same job field?
   - ❏ Distinctive skills and/or a specialized education you already possess
   - ❏ A genuine love of the job field
   - ❏ The salary your job field offers
   - ❏ Other: _____

3. Are you poised and ready for a complete job sea change? _____

4. Are you willing and able to work in a different job field? _____

5. If you are, do you have any particular areas in mind? _____

6. What are they? _____

7. Is a business of your own something you've always wanted? _____

8. Is being your own boss practical considering your current life circumstances (family responsibilities, finances, etc.)? _____

9. Are you open to just about *anything*—a new job, career, or business in whatever strikes your fancy or comes your way? _____

10. Are you prepared to re-enter the "traditional" working environment? _____

11. Does a "nontraditional" working situation sound tempting? _____

12. Do you really want to work at all? _____

Thoughtful answers to these questions will expose your unique bottom line as it relates to your particular destiny. In point of fact, there are innumerable unemployment turnaround stories in Jobless Land. There are countless people who fast found themselves swept up by something totally new, exciting, and rewarding. Indeed, a spanking new job, career, or business—that only yesterday you never saw coming—could be in your crystal ball. But then again, maybe that's not at all what you desire. Whatever scenario eventually plays out, you want to be able to say, without any hesitation on your part, that having been jobless is what augured your new beginning and bestowed upon you the ultimate unemployment benefit.

Worst-case Scenarios Often Aren't that Bad

Before you can spank the bottom of your job loss progeny—your *new beginning*—you've naturally got to confront head-on a stable of very understandable fears. To help you accomplish this not inconsiderable task, let us return to the college classroom for one last lesson—specifically, to a course called Essentials in Marketing. The instructor is a man by the name of Dr. Andre San Augustine. And one of the course's requirements is the dreaded oral presentation.

Dr. San Augustine fully appreciates that human nature equates a speech in front of a group of people as something on par with crossing the ocean in a leaky skiff, facing a firing squad, or, perhaps, eating a live scorpion to survive in the tradition of Bear Grylls. So, prior to his students delivering their respective presentations, the professor poses this question as the crux of his lecture: "What's the worst thing that can possibly happen to you while making your presentation?" He adds, "You're not going to die." And so it goes with your myriad jobless fears. *You're not going to die.*

That said, now is as good a time as any for you to identify your innumerable unemployment fears and link each one—very specifically—with what you deem a worst-case scenario. By completing this somewhat involved and thoughtful exercise, you'll more than likely be surprised that the worst-case scenarios envisioned are often not that bad. Before proceeding with this assignment, contemplate these three generally accepted truths:

1. **You are among a longstanding fraternity—the unemployed.** You are not alone in being jobless in the here and now. And recorded history is chock full of persons who lost their livelihoods and then made some nifty rebounds.

2. **There are solutions to virtually every problem that you encounter.** If you do what you have to do in confronting each one of them (and, granted, some of these solutions may not be especially appetizing as they relate to your psyche and pride), you'll make it to the *other side* in one piece. (And you won't need John Edward to conjure up your late Aunt Hazel or your childhood teddy bear to get you there.)

3. **Adversity more often than not makes us stronger and more resilient human beings.** You'll be alive and well when you get your next job, forge a new career, or start a fresh business.

EXERCISE
Let Go and Go Forward

It's critical that you both get over the loss of your previous job and begin hunting for your next one psychologically unshackled. What follows is a series of questions that'll assist you in coming to terms with the particulars that you didn't like about your last job or career path. Simultaneously, your answers will shine light on the very things that you want to steer clear of in your next employment incarnation:

1. What prescribed job tasks did you least appreciate in your last place of employment?_____

2. What work relationships did you find counterproductive?

   _____

3. What aspects of your compensation did you think were sub-par?_____

4. What job responsibilities did you consider too great? Too trifling?_____

5. What job roles did you play that were underappreciated or unappreciated altogether? _____

6. What else bugged you about your last job? _____

   _____

   _____

   _____

   _____

   (If there aren't enough lines here, feel free to continue your list on the back pages of this book ... and breathe a sigh of relief that you escaped from that horrible time-suck of a job in one piece.)

If you honestly and thoroughly answer these questions, you'll have the written evidence you need to divorce yourself from your past employment and plot your future with confidence.

Unemployment Benefit #2

Instead of being a bit player in your co-workers' decidedly uninteresting soap operas, you can watch more compelling soap operas on television.

EXERCISE
Jobless Fear Factor: Worst-case Scenarios

This exercise is divided into the five categories listed below. It asks that you put down on paper your biggest fear or fears as it relates to each one of them. After enumerating your fears under the various classifications, connect them—one by one—with what you deem a *realistic* worst-case scenario that could arise (e.g., FEAR: Won't be able to pay next month's rent on time. WORST-CASE SCENARIO: Landlord will harass me with phone calls).

To assist you in this exercise, ask yourself questions like these to first identify your fears and then facilitate the painting of your worst-case scenario pictures:

Financial Obligations

1. For how long can I meet my financial responsibilities without a source of income?

   _____

2. Where can I generate part-time income while simultaneously looking for a full-time job?

   _____

3. If need be, do I know people who could lend me money in a pinch?

   _____

4. What are the areas in my life where I can make sacrifices to tide me over until I find work?

   _____

Personal Relationships

5. Will my family and friends support me emotionally in forging a new start?

   _____

6. Do I know people who can help me find my next job, career, or a worthwhile business opportunity?

   _____

7. How will a temporary loss of income impact the various relationships in my life?

   _____

Health and Wellness

8. Will my health suffer when I am unemployed because of lifestyle changes?

   _____

9. Will I be able to maintain medical coverage when I'm out of work?

_____

Job Safari Pitfalls

10. Will my current skills be enough to land me a quality job in the near future?

_____

11. Am I emotionally ready to make a big job or career change?

_____

Competitive Edge

12. Am I sharp enough to beat out the stiff competition for good jobs?

_____

13. Have my interview skills gotten rusty?

_____

If You Think You Have It Bad...

In the rooms of many twelve-step programs, sentiment like this is regularly spoken: "The worst problem in the room is yours—because it's happening to *you*." In other words, you may hear a heaping helping of horror stories from others—folks who have had and have it much rougher than you do—but, still, your little sliver of the world and particular problems matter a whole lot more to you. And while you may supremely empathize with your fellow weary world travelers, the problems that hit home the hardest are understandably your own.

Nevertheless, the expression "Misery loves company" resonates with us when we are down and knocked for a loop. So, while we are wading through the important bailiwick of this thing called attitude, we'd be remiss by not prying open the "If You Think You Have It Bad" file and revisiting the Great Depression, a time in our nation's history (and indeed the world's history) when unemployment, underemployment, and widespread despair were omnipresent. Chew on these stubborn facts:

✦ In 1933, unemployment hit 24.9 percent of the population.

✦ Between 1929 and 1933, money supply contracted 31 percent.

✦ More than 10,000 banks failed between 1929 and 1933. This figure represented 40 percent of the total number of lending institutions.

✦ Thousands of depositors lost their life savings due to bank failures—to the tune of $2 billion!

✦ In 1933, President Franklin Roosevelt declared a bank holiday to cut short a run on banks by panicked depositors.

✦ Industrial stock prices lost more than 80 percent of their value between 1929 and 1933.

✦ The nation's Gross National Product (GNP) fell 31 percent in the first four years of this economic descent to end all economic descents.

Perhaps you can take a smidgen of succor in knowing that the jobless environment in which you presently find yourself—which, to be sure, is no bed of roses—is nonetheless a whole lot more hospitable than it was during the Great Depression years. And you won't need to sell apples and lead pencils on the street—as some forlorn folks did in those days of yore—to earn a few hard-to-come-by pennies, nickels, and dimes. Among today's multiple income-generating possibilities, you can sell things on eBay, for instance, to narrow any financial gaps generated by your unemployment. If you qualify, you can receive unemployment insurance. There are job fairs to help you locate work. The list goes on and on. In fact, there are more helping hands around these days than ever before, and we'll be enumerating both what they are and where they can be accessed throughout the pages of this book—so, by all means, keep reading.

Feel Proud to Be a Jobless Statistic

As previously noted, you are in esteemed company as a charter member in good standing of the Jobless Society. Joblessness happens to the best of us. It is not quite the ultimate equalizer that death is, but it's pretty darn egalitarian when it puts out its well-tread welcome mat. Look upon unemployment as an adult worker bee's rite of passage. Wear your unemployment status with pride, because there's absolutely nothing to be ashamed of.

What Do You Do Now?

We are very often defined by what we *do* in life—by our jobs, careers, or businesses. Our workload is who we are in the probing eyes of many others, and little else matters. And so, not surprisingly, unemployment raises a few self-esteem concerns. What if, God forbid, someone asks you what you *do*, or how you earn your living, when you're living the life of an intrepid job or career *seeker*? Here are some possible answers to that oft-posed question:

✦ *I'm between jobs* (a safe and benign old favorite).

✦ *I'm looking for a better-paying job* (bland but truthful in many instances).

✦ *I'm plotting my next career move* (rings a touch more active and bolder to the ears).

✦ *I'm presently a jobless statistic* (which you are).

✦ *I've been downsized to a couch potato* (sad but true).

✦ *I'm tired of paying taxes and thought I'd take a time-out from earning taxable income* (a capital idea).

✦ *I thought I'd use some of my retirement time while I still have my own teeth* (solid food for thought).

✦ *I'm in a work stoppage* (who could argue with that?).

✦ *I'm an unemployment benefits collector* (if the shoe fits . . .).

✦ *I'm a jobless engineer seeking a change in careers* (a noble endeavor).

Unemployment: Membership Has Its Privileges

Men and women who have taken a life blow or two (or three) are more apt to experience the greatest career successes, instances of personal redemption, and other lofty life feats. History tells us as much. In life, you have to be tested to earn your flight wings, so to speak. With a little adversity to draw on as your energy source, you are more likely to be a life achiever than somebody who has known no crises or encountered no real obstacles.

That said, if you consider your unemployment status as loaded with benefits beyond a government paycheck, you'll parry this life blow with the dexterity of Muhammad Ali in his prime. You are in essence a survivor on the Jobless Island. But in your very own personal reality show, you want to be voted off this island—eventually, at least. Being the last man or woman standing in the sand is not the prize. Leaving in one piece, better for having weathered the jobless time spent, is your ultimate goal. What's imperative is that you scrupulously look for the potential benefits of unemployment while you're unemployed, because they really do exist.

EXERCISE
Membership Has Its Privileges and "Unemployment Benefits"

1. Are you spending more time with and getting to better know members of your family circle (husband, wife, children, et al)? _____

2. Are you saving money courtesy of no longer commuting to work? (Fewer gasoline purchases amounts to *not* feathering the nests of OPEC members, enhancing oil company bottom lines, and contributing to obscene executive bonuses.) _____

3. Are you catching up on your sleep (which scientists say is essential to healthier living)? _____

4. Are you seeing and getting to know neighbors with whom you rarely spoke previously (or whom you never even knew were your neighbors)? _____

5. Are you exercising more courtesy of your newfound flexible schedule—perhaps going to the gym, jogging, bicycling, or taking long walks? _____

6. Are you eating better—more healthy foods in less stressful settings—than when you were on the job? (Polishing off a greasy sandwich at your desk at work or purchasing fare at a fast-food joint during a harried lunch break is a recipe for clogged arteries and every conceivable ailment.) _____

7. Are you discovering the artist within you by working on craft projects or other artistic endeavors that you never had the time for before? _____

8. Are you taking note of the little things in life that you never noticed in your fast and furious world of work, work, work? _____

9. Are you taking an interest in community affairs and local issues that you never previously contemplated or had the time for? _____

10. Are you finally free from the tyranny of an unappreciative and parsimonious employer? _____

If you answered yes to one or more of the above questions, you've uncovered some of the benefits of being unemployed— and there are many more where those came from!

Survivors: A Who's Who of the Formerly Unemployed

As a dues-paying member of the unemployment fraternity, you are in the company of more than a few good men and women. Recruitment, in fact, is multiplying like rabbits as you read these words. In addition, the alumni in this esteemed assemblage are at once a numerous and remarkably diverse cast of characters. (We've briefly touched on this very subject in this chapter—i.e., that you are not alone in your jobless straits—but it pays to drive this point home.)

Yes, their names are legion—both the present unemployed as well as the formerly unemployed. So, to tie a neat bow around this chapter about the importance of a positive attitude—while simultaneously paying homage to the celebrity culture in which we live—we're going to exhume a sundry crop of currently famous folks who previously experienced a moment or two as jobless statistics. Again, what their individual stories underscore is that prosperity—to paraphrase the lamented President Herbert Hoover—is often just around the corner. But, just like the stars of the down-and-out-nonentity-to-well-to-do-celebrity tales you're about to encounter, you too have got to keep on walking the straight and narrow, accentuating the positive along the way, until you reach that corner.

Now, let's have a little fun here and permit several formerly jobless souls—who are now familiar faces (or familiar names, at least)—to introduce themselves to us in the tradition of the long-running, immensely popular, and historic game show known as *What's My Line*. You are hereby christened a panelist in *What's My Unemployment Line*, and your job is to hazard a guess, based on their individual tales from the jobless side of the tracks, who each one of these formerly unemployed—and now prominent—men and women is.

What's my unemployment line?

My savings are nearly depleted. A nest egg for the future is nowhere to be found—there's barely an embryo of savings in the bank. On past tax returns dating back almost two decades, my occupation is listed as "actor." But, alas, my phone is not ringing off the hook with job offers.

So, what's shocking about this scenario, you ask? Doesn't the preponderance of the population of California consist of aspiring actors and actresses? Perhaps, but the reality is that I'm living in a truck bed camper in the golden state's San Fernando Valley. What galls me is that I, only recently, boldly went where no man has gone before. And now I'm compelled to take any job that comes my way—even appearing at private parties—just to pay my bills and support my family.

Care to hazard a guess as to who I am?

I'm **William Shatner**, Captain James T. Kirk of the Starship Enterprise. And yes, things got pretty bad for me after *Star Trek* was cancelled. The Trekkie phenomenon didn't take flight until years later, courtesy of the show being discovered by the masses in reruns. I now refer to my jobless stint as "that period." But look how things turned out. You know me now as Denny Crane on *Boston Legal* and the peripatetic spokesperson in Priceline commercials.

What's my unemployment line?

To live closer to my sister, I have just moved from Portugal to Edinburgh, Scotland. Born and raised in England, I recently ventured to Portugal to teach English as a foreign language. While living there, I met a Portuguese television journalist, married him, and had a child. Our marriage, however, was short-lived and we separated.

Sans both a marriage and a job, and with a daughter to raise on my own, I try to get my life in order. I have long fancied myself a gifted writer and have been developing a multi-layered fantasy story about a young boy with certain innate qualities beyond the capacity of mere mortals like us. I want to complete the manuscript now more than ever and see it published in book form someday. I apply for a governmental grant to help me do this. The Scottish government comes through with a helping hand—and their modest munificence enables me to see the project through to its conclusion.

During this topsy-turvy period of time, I am also diagnosed with clinical depression and receive government assistance to help me pay my bills. With my finished book manuscript now making the rounds in literary circles, I receive several rejections, which are never welcome salutations. Finally, the children's book division of the British company Bloomsbury agrees to publish my book in the United Kingdom. American rights to the title are subsequently purchased by Scholastic, which introduces my work to the vast readership in the land of the free and home of the brave.

Care to hazard a guess as to who I am?

I'm **J. K. Rowling**, author of the *Harry Potter* fantasy series of books. Things looked pretty grim for a spell. But I endured and the breaks started coming my way. I am now one of the wealthiest people in world. *Forbes* magazine says that I'm the first person to reach the billionaire stratosphere *solely* by writing books. Not bad for a formerly unemployed person collecting welfare.

What's my unemployment line?

I am living in an apartment with no furniture to speak of and no telephone. I dropped out of high school to forge a career as an actor. I repeatedly go to auditions, but don't know how much longer I can survive in my present state of increasingly conspicuous deprivation. I desperately need a well-paying job.

Fortunately, one particular audition offers me a glimmer of hope. I'm told that NBC is seriously considering me for a starring role in a new sitcom, and that they'll be calling me with a decision shortly. But the trouble is: I don't have a phone! I'm compelled by necessity to give them the number of a phone booth near my less than humble abode, pretending it's my home phone. I tell the folks at the network to call me between the hours of four and five o'clock in the afternoon—when I'm home from my busy day. (The scenario just laid out, believe it or not, took place before answering machines became commonplace, let alone voicemail and cell phone technology, which were more than a decade down the road.)

Camping out in the phone booth for the specified time period, I actually get the call I've been hoping and praying for, and am offered a part in a television sitcom. It subsequently becomes a big hit. Simultaneously, I also star in a few big screen blockbusters.

Care to hazard a guess as to who I am?

I'm **Michael J. Fox**, star of *Family Ties* and the *Back to the Future* movie trilogy. I was jobless and broke when I landed the role of Alex Keaton in *Family Ties*, which ran for seven years. Since that time, more than a quarter of a century ago, I've done lots of television and movies, including starring in the long-running, award-winning sitcom *Spin City*.

What's my unemployment line?

I've just been fired from my job for, in essence, talking too much and saying an impolitic thing or two. Funny, I'd been discharged from past positions for similar infractions. But, I suppose, that's the nature of the industry I work in.

I must admit that during these stretches of joblessness, things occasionally got pretty tight for me. I once visited a convenience store to buy a few needed grocery items, tried to pay with my credit card, and had the plastic money chopped up in front of me—as well as fellow store patrons—by an overly conscientious clerk.

Never one to throw in the towel in the field I always wanted to make a name in, I get another job. Things work out a little better for me during this go around. For one, I no longer employ a name that's not my own—like Rusty Sharpe or Jeff Christie. Now I can be my own man and host a radio program where expressing my opinions is what I get paid to do, and saying an impolitic thing or two won't get me fired.

Care to hazard a guess as to who I am?

I am **Rush Limbaugh**, immensely popular and always controversial host of *The Rush Limbaugh Show*, a nationally syndicated radio broadcast heard all across the fruited plain. From as long as I can remember, I always wanted to be a successful radio deejay. I persevered through periodic firings and joblessness to become the undisputed king of talk radio.

What's my unemployment line?

I've just been let go from my first reporting job because while covering stories I was less than successful at masking my emotions and keeping my personal opinions at arm's length. And not to pile on here, but I've had a pretty rough upbringing. As a young girl, I took solace in assuming the imaginary role of interviewer by probing the hearts and souls of my corncob doll and the vociferous and curious pack of crows that regularly visited my family home.

But my aforementioned job loss doesn't get me down—it is merely a temporary blip on my career radar. In fact, it serves as a bridge to what I really want to do and what I am most qualified to do.

Care to hazard a guess as to who I am?

I am **Oprah Winfrey**, multiple Emmy Award–winning host of *The Oprah Winfrey Show*, the highest-rated talk show in the annals of television. I am also the first African American billionaire, not to mention a brand unto myself. I firmly believe that "luck is a matter of preparation meeting opportunity."

What's my unemployment line?

I marry my drug counselor, who most definitely helped me kick a habit that would have eventually cast me asunder, and then I divorce him. I am jobless for occasional stretches of time. I am also the recipient of governmental assistance at various points in my early adult life. Intermingled with my unemployment episodes are a panoply of jobs, including working in a funeral parlor prettying up the dearly departed, sweating profusely as a bricklayer under the baking hot sun, washing dishes in a fast-food joint, and counting out money in the guise of bank teller.

Although I toil in a variety of lowly jobs, my life goal is to become a comedienne and actress someday. And through all of my trials and tribulations, I never lose faith that my heartfelt goal will be realized. Eventually,

I help found the San Diego Repertory Company. It is there that I take an unusual stage name that sticks to me like glue—whoopee!

Care to hazard a guess as to who I am?

I am Caryn Johnson, better known as **Whoopi Goldberg**. I am one of only four actresses to have won an Emmy, Grammy, Oscar, and Tony. I have also attained a prominent seat on *The View*—a not-too-shabby résumé for an unemployment alumnus.

Sure, we've just focused our rhetorical howitzers on celebrities, mainly amid the glitter and glare of Tinseltown. There are, however, untold business success stories that are the offspring of struggle, including periodic and, in some instances, lengthy periods of unemployment and all of the uncertainties and high anxieties that come with it.

Take **Ray Kroc**, the man who transformed a fast-food hamburger restaurant into an international phenomenon and one of the most identifiable brands on the planet. He wasn't born with a silver spoon in his mouth—not even a plastic one. Kroc grew up in Chicago, Illinois, the son of Czech immigrants, and toiled in every job imaginable, including paper-cup salesman and piano player. He lost many jobs and experienced bouts of unemployment.

Ray Kroc eventually became a traveling salesman who extolled the mind-blowing virtues of multi-mixer machines. This particular job brought him into contact with two brothers: Richard and Maurice McDonald, the founders of the original McDonald's fast-food restaurant. Let's just say that the rest is history …

Meanwhile, **Milton Hershey**, born on a small farm in Pennsylvania Dutch Country, quit school with only a fourth-grade education under his belt. As a youth, he served in an apprenticeship with a Lancaster, Pennsylvania printer, but lost his position when he purposely permitted his hat to tumble into a printing press, wreaking havoc on the job at hand. Subsequently, he served as an apprentice with a maker of candies. Years later, he tried his hand at a candy-making business of his own, then another and another after that with less than sweet results. But Milton Hershey persevered. Ever hear of Hershey's chocolates? How about Hershey, Pennsylvania?

Joblessness happens to a cross-section of one and all in the twenty-first century, just as it did in the days of yore. For most people, unemployment is just a blip—a learning experience—ushering in a new chapter in their lives. By maintaining a positive attitude during your joblessness, you are most definitely poised on the precipice of something new and exciting. So, just roll with the punches, and you'll not only elude the jabs that come your way, but you'll end up a stronger, more durable fighter for future bouts.

Unemployment Funnies

Come hell or high water, it pays to maintain a sense of humor in life. Death and dying are fodder for all kinds of jokes. So, it should come as no surprise to you that job loss and stretches of unemployment spur their share of humorous anecdotes, one-liners, and jokes. Just remember the old saying, "Laugh and the whole world laughs with you; cry and you cry alone."

Unemployment Sleep Number

What's your unemployment sleep number? In case you're wondering, this number has nothing to do with the squishy quality, or lack thereof, of your mattress. It refers to how many hours of sleep you get courtesy of not having to go to work in the morning. So, what is it: ten, twelve, fourteen?

Lost and Found

The truth is sometimes stranger than fiction. Ted gets the bad news that he's just been laid off. He meets his longtime co-worker, Paul, in the hallway shortly thereafter. Noticing something amiss, Paul asks: "What's wrong? You look like you've just seen Lord Voldemort." Ted answers, "I've just lost my job." Matter-of-factly, Paul responds, "It'll probably turn up in lost and found—everything else does." (Paul, an allergy sufferer with perpetually clogged ears, obviously lost something in the congested translation.)

Embarrassing Moment

"Hey, your pink slip is showing!" Don't let this happen to you. Dress for success, even when jobless—even if you're purchasing your clothes at a Salvation Army thrift shop.

New Age Joblessness

Spotted on the highways and byways are wearers of T-shirts sporting such slogans as:

+ Will Work for a Tofu Hotdog
+ Will Work for an iPod
+ Will Work for a Panini Sandwich
+ Will Work for a Peppermint Latte
+ Will Work for a Fuzzy Peach Smoothie

Unemployment Inflation

During the Great Depression, the query made legendary by desperate jobless souls was: "Brother, can you spare a dime?" That same question today—adjusted for inflation—would be: "Brother, can you spare $1.20?" or, on second thought, "Brother or sister, can you spare $1.20?"

There's Always a Bright Side

For women on the unemployment rolls, look on the bright side of joblessness: There are no glass ceilings where you stand now.

Unemployment Benefits ... German Style

The world's oldest profession is perfectly legal in Germany. Located next door to an unemployment office, one particular firm in this resilient profession offers healthy discounts to the jobless minions. One unemployed fellow—and highly satisfied patron—remarks at his good fortune: "Before I could only have my fun once every couple of months, if that. But now I can go twice a month for a rock-bottom price, and the quality of the service still remains the same." An employee of the firm confirms the customer's assessment: "We give them the same service, just without the long talks that we usually do to get a client going. At that price we can't afford to waste that much time."

Tax Deferment

So, you finally found a foolproof way to reduce your tax burden and stick it to the IRS. Losing your job is a sure-fire tax saver every time.

Politicians Say the Darndest Things

When it comes to unemployment, politicians are known to weigh in. Harry Truman once said, "It's a recession when your neighbor loses his job; it's a depression when you lose your own." Former British Prime Minister Edward Heath opined that "unemployment is of vital importance, particularly to the unemployed." A truer statement was never uttered. "In the long run, the right answer to unemployment is to create more jobs," said George W. Bush during a presidential radio address. Who can argue with that logic?

New World in the Morning

Losing your job, or voluntarily leaving a job you didn't much care for, has been known to cure morning sickness. It's also been known to combat rude awakenings. When you've long equated the rooster's clarion call with a day of drudgery, unemployment removes the equivalent of a daily hangover.

PART ONE

TAKING CONTROL

CHAPTER

ONE

Getting the Unpleasant Stuff Out of the Way

The trouble with unemployment
is that the minute you wake up in the morning, you're on the job.

—Slappy White, comedian

I f you've already taken care of the laborious jobless minutiae—applying for unemployment benefits, resolving severance issues, and so on—then by all means leap ahead in the book to the sunny side of the street. The heart and soul of the pages to follow are all about converting unemployment lemons into refreshing and enjoyable lemonade. In other words, in addition to searching for another line of work, you can savor a full glass of fun and frolic as well. If, on the other hand, you need an unemployment roadmap, we've got that too.

So, if you need a little assistance in getting your jobless ducks in a row, start by submitting a claim for unemployment insurance. Granted, not everyone qualifies for these state-administered benefits, but if you've been fired, laid off, downsized, outsourced—or whatever particular euphemism applies to your involuntary loss of a paying job—you more than likely meet the criteria for unemployment compensation.

However, keep in mind that not everyone is created equal in the eyes of this bureaucratic lifeline. In other words, the generosity or lack thereof of jobless benefits varies from state to state. In addition, the paycheck that you will ultimately receive—if, of course, you meet your state's myriad eligibility requirements—is effectively linked to what you've most recently earned in paying jobs throughout the past year. This is known as the *base period* in unemployment jargon.

So, to put unemployment compensation into a broader perspective: If you were taking home $450 a week and your neighbor, who just lost her job, pulled down $1,200 a week, it's a safe bet that the size of your two unemployment checks would differ. In fact, your check would more than likely be a Mini Me version of your neighbor's. But there are rather low ceilings on the upper limits of jobless benefits paid out, regardless of where you live. Each of the fifty states has a maximum figure threshold for its unemployment compensation. And let's just say that some of these maximum numbers are rather minimum. In other words, even if you were making $2,000 a week and apply for an unemployment check, there's only so much you can get.

Now, before we venture any further in this subject matter, it's time to disabuse those of you who have never before waded into unemployment insurance waters. Your jobless benefits will *not* equal—or even come reasonably close—to what you earned on a weekly basis in your last job, or the weekly average of the multiple jobs you have held in the past year. It's just not how the system works. As previously indicated, the individual states have ceilings on the top dollar amount that you can receive—and they vary considerably. Depending on where you call home, as well as your past income numbers, it is not unusual to see unemployment benefits tally up to approximately half of your recent earnings.

With this necessary disclaimer out of the way, it is nevertheless a fact of life that unemployment checks are big—*really big*—for most recipients of them. Very often receipt of jobless benefits is the difference between you subsisting on a daily repast of no-frills canned soups and hamburger helper versus eating the occasional piece of chicken and Dunkin' Donuts for dessert—not to mention being able to pay your utility bills, the monthly car payment, and, of course, the rent or mortgage. So, while an unemployment check is not—by any stretch of the imagination— comparable to a full-time job paycheck, it's often substantial in light of your out-of-work financial straits. When your income is at ground zero, jobless benefits—at whatever level—are very welcome indeed.

Unemployment Insurance: Are You a Candidate?

For openers, there are two websites worth checking out: the U.S. Department of Labor at dol.gov (1-877-US-2JOBS) and CareerOne Stop.org (1-877-348-0502), which is sponsored by the former. These cyber portals furnish links to the fifty states and their respective labor departments. They are also replete with information on employment services and other job-related issues that you might find useful, includ- ing comprehensive job banks that can aid and abet your work safari. Of course, if you are from the old school, you could directly contact your local unemployment claims office by opening up the yellow pages and letting your fingers do the walking.

It makes little difference what methodology brings you to your state's unemployment insurance division. Once there—via a website, telephone call, or in-person visit—you'll be outfitted with all of the rules and regulations that you must abide by to qualify for a regular unemployment check. Federal guidelines exist that mandate all fifty states do certain prescribed things vis-à-vis unemployment insurance—like having a program to begin with—but it's the individual state governments that determine most of the particulars, including:

+ Eligibility requirements
+ Duration of the benefits paid out
+ Amount of benefits formulae
+ Maximum benefits paid out
+ Job search reporting requirements.

The Filing Process

Courtesy of the highly advanced technological and super-automated age that we live in, filing for—and indeed collecting—unemployment benefits has gotten a whole lot simpler. Ordinarily, unemployment insurance claims can be applied for over the telephone or online. In the not too distant past, applications were completed and submitted in-person at unemployment claims offices near you, which often entailed long waits in even longer lines and, worse yet, interaction with beleaguered bureaucrats who always seemed like they'd rather be in another line of work—or, perhaps, jobless themselves. And, here's the kicker: you had to repeat this process week after week after week to continue qualifying for your checks. This grueling system added an unnecessarily demeaning layer to already rough roads.

Consider yourself extremely fortunate then that you can keep visits to the unemployment claims office to a bare minimum. (As a recipient of jobless benefits, you may at some point have to make a personal appearance at a physical location and speak to a flesh-and-blood human being. You might have to furnish proof of your past income sources, or clarify something else on your initial application. It could be that, after you're approved, you'll have to update the powers that be on your job search progress. But most of these matters can be handled over the telephone or online.)

In any event, your state unemployment insurance division will fill you in on exactly what you need to do along the way—from filing for the initial benefits to maintaining your weekly or, in some cases, biweekly checks. More or less, the filing process unfolds this way in all quarters of the country:

1. You submit an application through the proper channels, either by phone, the Internet, or in-person at a local unemployment claims office.

2. You furnish proof that you are who you say you are; your social security number will suffice.

3. You provide a home address with a zip code and a telephone number where you can be reached.

4. You furnish proof of your past employer or employers over the past year, including names, addresses, and dates of employment. What you earned during this time frame will fundamentally determine the amount of your unemployment check.

5. You begin actively looking for a job.

Frequently Asked Questions about Unemployment Insurance

When should I file for unemployment benefits?

You should file for unemployment compensation the moment you find yourself a jobless statistic. The stark reality is that even if your claim is approved lickety-split, you won't receive your first check for at least two weeks and probably longer than that.

Do I have to look for work while receiving jobless benefits?

Yes, but of course it's in your best interests to be proactive in your job or career search anyway. Many states require that recipients of unemployment benefits register with a state job service, or at least avail themselves of its resources. In some instances—depending on your previous line of work and past income—you may be *required* to apply for certain jobs and submit résumés to specified employers, or risk having your benefits discontinued. There are circumstances that occasionally arise when you are asked to take a particular job. That is, your choice is to take the position, or turn it down and lose your unemployment compensation.

Will I have to show proof that I've been actively looking for another job?

Most states require that the unemployed minions who receive jobless benefits reveal the fruits of their labors, as it were, regarding looking for work. This may entail you furnishing the unemployment claims office with lists of places you've submitted your résumés, as well as any job interviews you attended. In addition, you are expected to report any job offers that come your way, even if you pass on them.

How long can I expect to receive unemployment insurance?

Assuming that you cannot find suitable work that pays you a living wage, the maximum time allowed for receiving *standard* unemployment benefits is twenty-six weeks—approximately six months. In certain instances, there are extensions of up to thirteen weeks, and even thirteen weeks after that. Check with your unemployment insurance division to see if extended benefits are an option for your particular circumstances in your particular state. (Areas of the country with high unemployment are more likely to have provisions for extended benefits than areas enjoying low unemployment.)

Do I have to pay income taxes on my jobless benefits?

Sad to be the bearer of bad news here, but the answer is yes. Uncle Sam treats your unemployment check like any other earned income. So, be prepared to ante up to the taxman. When filing your unemployment benefits claim, you are given the option—upon approval—to have the government withhold the taxes at the time you receive your check, or you can defer the tax bite until you file your income taxes at the beginning of the next calendar year. The latter choice will ensure you a somewhat juicier unemployment check, which will no doubt come in handy when you need it most. However, if you're still financially wobbly come next April 15, having to cough up monies to pay the IRS may not be desirable, let alone feasible.

Can I qualify for unemployment insurance if I quit my job?

More times than not the answer is no, but there are a cornucopia of exceptions. You may qualify for jobless benefits if you quit your position because of unsafe working conditions or a physically unhealthy working environment (handling cancer-inducing chemicals, for instance). An unexpected change in working conditions (e.g., an hours shift, additional work hours demanded of you, or a pay cut) that is detrimental to you and at cross-purposes with your familial responsibilities could make a case for unemployment insurance. A broken contract might also do the trick, if, for example, you signed onto a job expecting certain things that your employer later reneged on.

There are other reasons for quitting a job that are sometimes deemed justifiable by unemployment claims evaluators, including leaving a job to care for a sick relative, a loss of transportation (the only way you can get to work), family emergencies, and, of course, a serious illness of your own.

But it's worth noting that in this nebulous zone of collecting unemployment benefits, the burden of proof is on you—always. You will be charged with exploring every possible alternative before quitting your job. In cases involving trials and tribulations with your employer, you will be asked to submit proof that you deliberated with your boss and made good faith efforts to resolve the disagreements between you. In instances where illness is the issue—either your own or a family member's—medical evidence must be supplied to support your claim.

Can I qualify for unemployment insurance if I had been self-employed?

The answer is usually no, but there are—as in many other gray areas—extenuating circumstances that, depending on your state's eligibility requirements, could make you a contender for an unemployment check. Bear in mind that unemployment benefits are derived from payroll taxes specifically paid by employers. This is where the unemployment insurance dollars come from. As a self-employed individual, you have no employer who paid into the fund, nor did you contribute to it. This one-two punch works against you—and more often than not it's a knockout blow.

Are there any other reasons that could make me ineligible for jobless benefits?

In just about every government-administered program, the bureaucrats who manage them are in the business of turning away as many people as possible. And this guiding principle applies to the administration of unemployment insurance as well. Applicants are carefully vetted, which is understandable considering all of the fraud in government entitlement programs.

That said, reasons that would more than likely make you ineligible for jobless benefits include leaving a position voluntarily without sufficient cause (in the eyes of the keyboard punchers). For example, you left your job because you didn't like your boss, or the pay scale wasn't up to snuff. These may in fact be reasons enough to quit a job, but they are not reasons enough for unemployment claims analysts to hand you a check. Quitting work to tie the knot, or returning to school to further your education—noble endeavors both—won't cut the mustard either with the aforementioned adjudicators. And, finally, if you were sent packing for transgressions such as cooking the books, having your sticky fingers in the company till, or some other brand of misconduct, you will have a tough time convincing the unemployment insurance division that your heart is really pure and that you merit a weekly or biweekly check while you look for another job.

Negotiating and Collecting Severance Pay

Let's take a rare step backwards for this one time and one time only to address the matter of severance pay. Depending, of course, on the employer who hands you your walking papers, the nature of the job you held, the exact reason for your dismissal, and your length of service on the job, you may be offered a severance package. In addition, the particulars of this package may, believe it or not, be negotiable. And being that the severance pay scenario unfolds while you are still on the job—although by the skin of your teeth—it occurs prior to your filing for unemployment benefits.

Severance Pay ABCs

First of all, there is no existing law that mandates that an employer provide an employee being shown the exit with a severance package of any sort. Unless you physically signed a written contract or were led to believe otherwise—via a company manual, for instance—offering severance pay is a voluntary action on the part of an employer.

Scary concept! *Voluntary* action! You're no doubt wondering right now why any business entity, which is foremost interested in sweetening its bottom line, would bestow severance packages upon laid-off employees, when they are not legally required to do so. After all, the corporate throng is not generally known for practicing random acts of kindness, especially when it comes to men and women who are being ushered out their respective doors.

For our purposes here, let's paint with a broad brush and suppose that most large corporations, along with the people responsible for enforcing their various dictates, are cold-blooded animals. In other words, there must be something in it for them when they offer terminated employees severance packages, right? And the answer, of course, is yes—there is indeed something in it for them.

When employers tender their departing employees severance deals, their generosity—if you want to call it that—redounds to their benefit as well. A policy of furnishing severance packages to employees on the cusp of collecting unemployment checks works to their advantage in critical areas that will soon be apparent. While being on the receiving end of a severance deal elevates your spirits and helps you bridge the financial gap until you land your next job, your ex-employer enjoys a decidedly different kind of reward.

So, exactly what might a company want from you in exchange for a fair severance package? Above all else, your employer could desire that you—in your future role as former employee—remain silent as to the inner workings of the business operation that you recently exited. Many employees accrue a surfeit of knowledge about the goings-on and behind-the-scenes adventures of the companies they work for. And this often includes important information on strategic planning for both the short- and the long-term. From your employer's perspective, this level of information is best kept on the inside where it belongs.

Keeping you away from the welcoming arms of the competition is another weighty benefit your employer could derive from offering you a decent severance deal. As a one-time employee running free and loose in the wider world, you are potentially a ticking time bomb awaiting full-blown detonation in your erstwhile employer's face. That is, of course, only if you are scooped up and deprogrammed by a direct competitor.

In the dog-eat-dog business world, these kinds of justifiable fears compel many companies to offer severance packages that are tied together not with pretty red bows, but stringent understandings instead. In other words, if you want the dough, your employer wants your John Hancock on a document extracting a promise or two from you. In many instances, it all boils down to your employer wanting your silence. Not unlike the mafia, "mum's the word" is a very big deal in the inner sanctums of the ultra-competitive environment that is corporate America.

The wording in a severance pay agreement might ask you to keep your yap shut about this, that, and the other thing vis-à-vis the competition, or forbid you to discuss the company in any way, shape, or form on a YouTube video, in Internet chat rooms, or in any other public venue. Negative publicity is the last thing a company wants. Depending on your exact job role, there are some agreements that would forbid you from assuming a physical job with a direct competitor; others could even prohibit you from laboring in the same industry—period—for two, three, or five years. These are popularly known as *non-compete clauses.*

And, finally, in this extraordinarily litigious age that we call home, yet another reason why your employer might offer you a respectable severance pay package is the company's very legitimate fear of being sued for workplace discrimination, or something else related to your dismissal. Legal suits between ex-employees and ex-employers are at once omnipresent and very expensive to litigate. Again, codicils to many severance packages contain releases for you to sign, where you promise not to initiate a lawsuit against your former employer.

What all of these concerns emanating from on high reveal is that you, in fact, have some serious leverage when it comes to the size and shape of your severance pay package. Depending on your particular circumstances, you might be able to negotiate a better deal for yourself. It's not, as all too many people assume, always a matter of "take it or leave it."

What's Negotiable in Severance Packages?

As there are no hard and fast rules ordaining the sizes of severance packages, likewise there are no hard and fast rules overseeing what exactly goes into them. The devil is in the details when it comes to your severance deal. Severance pay is not all about receiving a lump sum of money when you breathe your last for an employer. In addition to literal dollars greasing your palm, there are other concerns of some magnitude weighing on your shoulders when you exit a job, which are often negotiable, such as maintaining your company's contribution to medical coverage while you are looking for work.

In some instances, a letter of reference from your former boss to beef up your work portfolio is a nice parting volley and welcome severance particular. You could draft a reference letter, load it up with facts and a list of your many accomplishments, and ask your boss to sign it. This kind of thing is often negotiable during your parting of the ways, as are other items involving your job search, including access to outplacement resources and office and administrative support.

Another area of keen interest to you—and potentially negotiable—is the scheduled distribution of your severance benefits. Naturally, you want this evolutionary process to work in your favor and not against you in any way. Contemplate this food for thought: Some severance packages are dispensed over multiple months and preclude their recipients from collecting unemployment checks during this time period. Whereas, if the same package is dispensed with in one fell swoop at the moment of departure, its beneficiaries could apply for and receive unemployment compensation immediately.

As an appendage to the aforementioned negotiable areas, the reasons we've previously annotated as to why employers offer severance packages—i.e., to get something in return from their ex-employees—are also negotiable on certain points. The shock and awe of job loss can, quite understandably, render you a shivering heap. Legitimate fears can lead you to believe that you had better take what you can get and go quietly into the night. But remember, it's your future that's at stake here. You deserve to get what you can to facilitate a better tomorrow.

The Negotiating Process

When your employer offers you a severance package, you will, in most instances, have up to twenty-one, or perhaps as many as forty-five, days in which to accept or reject it. Federal law, in fact, mandates that such waiting periods be accorded all men and women over the age of forty. The law came into play after one-too-many laid-off persons—with the proverbial "take it or leave it" gun pointed at their heads—realized thereafter that they had completely signed away their legal right to sue for age discrimination, even though they fully believed that they were terminated because of the late hour of their biological clocks. In any event, most organizations that make severance packages available to employees give them the twenty-one or forty-five-day window to mull over the deal, regardless of the age of the dismissed party.

This period of weeks gives you ample time to pore over the severance package's fine print—from the actual dollar amount to health insurance issues to precisely the nature of the releases you are signing when accepting the offer. After contemplating the ABCs of the document, you can opt to accept or reject your employer's severance package at any point during the allotted time, and, if you so desire, you are entitled to make a counteroffer.

As an important footnote here, it's worth noting that a counteroffer on your part is considered a rejection of your employer's original severance package offer. Technically speaking, you are putting the whole enchilada at risk by making a counteroffer, because the original deal can be taken off the table entirely. So, yes, there is some risk involved in requesting a negotiation process—you could be left holding the contents of Charlie Brown's trick-or-treat bag—but, ordinarily, if your employer refuses to negotiate at all, or rejects your counteroffer, the original severance package remains a viable option.

Of course, the $64,000 question that looms like a colossus over this entire discussion is: What leverage do you have in negotiating a better severance deal than the one offered? After all, you're on your way out, so why exactly would a company care to wheel and deal with you on anything? The answer is that you've got a few cards to play that might be of interest to them. Again, it all boils down to why most employers offer severance packages in the first place. They want certain assurances from you in return for the severance pay.

EXERCISE
Severance Package Leverage: A Counteroffer Quiz

Before you consider making a counteroffer to your employer's original severance package deal, there are several questions you should ask yourself. Answers to these queries can clarify exactly what your tactic should be in going forward:

1. If you are part of a large-scale layoff, is there anything you can offer your employer that the others cannot (or have not thought to) offer?

    _____

2. Had you been led to believe when first assuming your position that it came with job security understandings that didn't pan out?

    _____

3. During your job tenure, were you involved in projects that were long-term in nature? (You may, in fact, have engaged in work that is ongoing and will benefit your employer long

after you are off the scene. This could mean that you are entitled to compensation of some kind—perhaps a bonus—for your contribution to its development.)

---

4. Do you have immediate financial needs and familial responsibilities that the loss of your job—and related benefits—could impact adversely? (There is nothing wrong with you appealing to the better angels of your employer to help you out at a difficult moment in your life. If, for instance, you have a spouse or child battling a serious illness, it behooves you to make your plight known and appeal to common decency. Even in the cold corporate climes that manifestly exist, there are some warm hearts amidst the many icebergs. Believe it or not, the very nature of this kind of appeal—highly personal—is often the strongest leverage you can have to enhance your severance package.)

---

5. Have you been the recipient of innuendo that may be behind your dismissal? (If losing your job is grounded in any way, shape, or form in what you deem defamation of character, make your feelings known to your employer, even if you are not claiming an outright violation of employment law.)

---

6. Do you think discrimination is behind your firing? (If you believe that age, race, or gender played a role in your dismissal, don't take it lying down. And this same reasoning applies to you losing your job on the eve of qualifying for certain benefits, for instance.)

The Negotiating Posture

When you've been handed a pink slip—no matter the reason behind it—it's a piercing body blow. Upon getting word of your impending ouster, your first reaction might be to burn down your company's office building or take your boss hostage. These are not recommended avenues to venture down, and they won't get you a better severance deal.

Seriously, you've got to fight off the urge to exact revenge on anybody. Approach severance negotiations like a levelheaded adult, which you are, and you'll benefit from the experience. In the business world, too, it's best not to burn bridges and develop a reputation for hotheadedness. You don't want to be known as the guy with the lawyer on retainer, either, just champing at the bit to commence a lawsuit.

This is not to say that initiating a lawsuit based on the facts is not worth pursuing. It certainly is! Just keep your actions rooted in the reality of your situation. Treat your soon-to-be-former employer fairly and you're more apt to be given a fair hearing—and, hopefully, a fair deal. Remember that most mid-sized and larger companies have the wherewithal to negotiate and furnish you with a better severance deal than the one originally offered. Your job is to make the case that you deserve it.

Remain composed during any negotiations and go for the gold, so to speak, regarding the contents of your severance package. If your employer consents to negotiations, the worst outcome is that your requests are denied. By keeping up a professional posture throughout the proceedings, win or lose, you come out ahead.

Hiring a Lawyer

Do you need an attorney to negotiate a severance package for you? Ordinarily the answer is no. Having a lawyer to litigate a court case is one kettle of fish, but it is not generally recommended in severance pay negotiations unless it's a particularly complicated deal. Bringing a lawyer into the negotiating process augurs an adversarial environment that might not be in your best interests. That is, the negotiations may change venues from the more sympathetic human resources department to the highly aggressive corporate legal department, which is more apt to play hardball. Leave the hardball-playing to Chris Matthews and Derek Jeter.

Still, you may find yourself in a situation where consulting legal counsel would benefit you, or would be absolutely needed, particularly if you feel you've been discriminated against and fired because of your age, race, or gender. This reasoning would also apply to your termination just before your pension benefits vest or some other accrued benefits are due.

To locate legal counsel in your backyard, you would do well to visit EmploymentIssues.com and FreeAdvice.com. Both websites feature comprehensive lawyer searches, which can pinpoint attorneys a hop, skip, and jump from your front door who specialize in employment-related matters. Both websites are chock-full of information on critical employment topics, including job termination issues and severance pay laws.

Losing Your Job, Keeping Your Health Coverage

In the preceding discussion on negotiating severance pay, we underscored why the continuation of your job-related health coverage is a benefit worth fighting for, if, in fact, it's not included in the original offer. On this particular playing field, it is critical that you know your rights with regards to health coverage continuity and purchasing health insurance during periods of unemployment, as well as the portability options that enable you to take your current medical plan from one job to another.

Acronym City

The U.S. Department of Labor through the Employee Benefits Security Administration (EBSA) oversees the Employee Retirement Income Security Act of 1974, more commonly known as ERISA. Under its vast umbrella, ERISA manages critical health coverage continuity concerns, including portability provisions as spelled out in the Consolidated Omnibus Budget Reconciliation Act, otherwise known as COBRA, and the Health Insurance Portability and Accountability Act, aka HIPAA.

For our purposes, what this sea of capital letters denotes is that when you lose your job, you shouldn't simultaneously lose your health insurance. You have certain rights, which amount to options in many instances to maintain your current health coverage or sidestep into a new plan without going uninsured for too long a period, if even for a single day. EBSA has a toll-free hotline: 1-866-444-3272. You can pose questions to the phone operators and, if you like, request free copies of beneficial publications, including one that addresses in detail health coverage for dislocated workers.

COBRA

What can COBRA do for you? Let us assume that your employer does not offer you a severance package with a temporary stay of your health coverage, or does not offer any severance at all. Federal law—via COBRA—mandates that companies that employ twenty or more persons offer their departing employees the option to continue in the company's group insurance plan. This means that you could keep your present coverage for the short-term future while you look for another job.

It is, in fact, the group insurance plan's responsibility to alert you—immediately upon word of your joblessness—of the available COBRA option and its costs. You then have sixty days to decide whether you want you to continue in the insurance plan. Even if your former employer is not contributing to your continued coverage while you are out of work, you will, nevertheless, be able to purchase its continuance at the established group rates—i.e., what companies pay to insure individuals in their workforces. This road enables you to remain in your former job's insurance plan and pay much more affordable premiums than you would otherwise—that is, if you had to purchase private health coverage on an individual basis.

When you accept COBRA coverage, it is always retroactive to the day you may have lost your insurance. COBRA coverage ordinarily lasts up to eighteen months, but there are extenuating circumstances when this time frame is extended.

Other Group Plans: Special Enrollment

Depending on your unique personal situation upon the loss of your job and corresponding medical coverage, a possible health insurance option is enrollment in your spouse's work-provided group plan. As you can ascertain from this scenario, two things need to be in place to make this a reality: a spouse and a spouse in a job with health coverage. Meet this personal profile, along with the plan's criteria, and you could find yourself in a very affordable segue from one major medical plan to another.

Federal dictates call this *special enrollment*, and it permits laid-off persons, who would ordinarily qualify for inclusion in their spouses' job-related health plans, but who chose not to participate in them (because of having separate coverage), to buy into them now. To meet the standard for special enrollment in a spouse's insurance plan, you must submit an application for coverage within a thirty-day window of losing prior coverage. If you opt to travel down this road and get approved from on high, the plan must ensure you insurance coverage by the first day of the first month after your application.

Unemployment Benefit #3

Courtesy of having no regular income, your tax bite is now considerably smaller.

Private Health Insurance

If you've lost your health insurance along with your job, see no COBRA option, and you don't have a partner with a plan you can join, you could purchase individual coverage via a private plan. For obvious reasons, this option is not the optimum one. In other words, it's often the costliest alternative available to you. And, when you're out of work, buying a comprehensive private health insurance policy could be beyond your financial means.

Nevertheless, keep in mind that private health insurers must guarantee you access to their plans, and cannot impose any pre-existing condition barriers, if you meet these four criteria:

1. You maintained health coverage for a minimum of eighteen months prior to applying for private insurance, and your coverage was in a group insurance plan.

2. Your group insurance coverage did not end because of either fraud on your part or missed premium payments.

3. You are ineligible for any kind of COBRA coverage, or have seen your COBRA coverage lapse.

4. You are not eligible for other forms of health insurance, such as COBRA or group coverage via an employer. (You're not working at the moment, so this shouldn't be too high a hurdle to leap over.)

Another category of private health coverage that could work for you during your jobless stretch is simply known as *temporary* or *short-term* insurance. These kinds of plans are offered to persons out of work, who are looking for a stopgap kind of coverage—something to tide them over until they land in a new job with medical benefits. By and large, these polices can be purchased for periods ranging from one month to one year.

By providing coverage for such limited time frames, temporary insurance plans are unquestionably cheaper to purchase. You might need a policy for three or four months—just in case something happens. So, this brand of medical coverage is crafted with you in mind. If you anticipate regaining more comprehensive, long-term coverage in the very near future, look into temporary insurance.

It's certainly worth noting that while offering significantly cheaper premiums, temporary insurance plans also have significantly higher deductibles. These kinds of policies in particular call upon you to scrupulously comb through the fine print. It's not unusual to encounter temporary insurance coverage with $2,000 to $3,000 deductibles, which means that you'd be paying out of pocket for just about all of your basic medical needs, save a hospital stay or catastrophic illness. But this kind of coverage may in fact be enough for you. That is, if you are foremost concerned with insurance against an unforeseen major medical incident that could take you to both the emergency room and the cleaners. After all, so many of us rarely, if ever, visit a doctor.

Explore Your Options

When you are out of a job, there are many options to explore with regard to the future of your health care coverage. A thorough website to peruse is the National Association of Health Underwriters (NAHU) at nahu.org. Here you'll come upon comprehensive databases in such categories as Employer-based Health Insurance, Individual Health Insurance Coverage, Assistance for Obtaining Health Coverage, and Health Care Coverage Contacts.

Finally, if things get really rough for you and you cannot afford health insurance through any of the aforementioned options, there are government assistance programs available. Contact the U.S. Department of Health and Human Services, Centers for Medicare and Medicaid Services at cms.gov, or call 410-786-1565.

Housing Decisions: The Roof Over Your Jobless Head

One of the biggest unemployment concerns hanging over your head is—quite literally—the roof over your head. While jobless, do you have the financial resources to keep yourself comfortably ensconced in your present home and hearth? As always, the answer to this question boils down to your unique circumstances, starting with how much you pay in monthly rent, building maintenance, or on a mortgage, what rainy day savings you have stashed in the kitty, and, last but not least, what viable alternatives you have for a more cost-friendly place to live.

The Landlord

For starters, if you lease an apartment and fall behind in your rent payments, the first thing you should do is speak with your landlord and explain your present unemployment straits. It can't hurt to lay your cards on the table, even if you—at this moment in time—have a losing hand. Naturally, for this scenario to play itself out, you must have a landlord who is a bona fide human being and not merely a post office box.

Enlightened landlords appreciate good tenants who pay their rent on time, don't throw wild parties, and keep complaints to a minimum. If this sounds like your tenant prototype, consider yourself as having a leg up. Your landlord just might cut you a break and permit you a little leeway in your rent payment schedule.

If, on the other hand, you absolutely feel that you cannot afford your current rent tab, and dread the prospects of falling into a subterranean hole from which you'll never get out, there are other options to weigh, including:

1. Taking in a roommate
2. Subletting your apartment (if allowed)
3. Temporarily moving in with family or friends
4. Finding a cheaper place to call home
5. Relocating altogether, perhaps to a different region of the country with more hospitable housing costs.

Tenant Rights

And if by chance you don't have one of those enlightened landlords just mentioned—and things get a little contentious between the two of you during your jobless stint—keep in mind that you have rights as a tenant. Although state laws vary on some of the particulars, you cannot be kicked out on the street without having your day in court. As you can surmise, too, this legal process doesn't commence and conclude overnight. It's a protracted affair.

Your landlord would have to first petition for a court hearing, which entails quite a bit of paperwork, serve you with the notice, and then wait for a scheduled hearing. In the end, your landlord must sue you in a legal proceeding and hope that the court grants an eviction request. So, it's not surprising that most landlords would prefer to deal with you—particularly if you're a good egg who experienced a bad break—rather than enter the labyrinthine halls of justice. On top of everything else, legal proceedings are quite costly with no guarantees of the final outcome.

The bottom line is that it's against the law for a landlord to forcibly evict a tenant. In other words, you can't be locked out of your apartment. Your utilities can't be turned off. Your landlord can't steal your belongings in lieu of rent payments. And, this is important, your landlord can't send a Luca Brasi type to your door either. If any of these threatening actions do come to pass, you've got a solid legal case against your landlord.

For a full plate of information on tenant rights and the many landlord-tenant particulars, visit RentLaw.com. This website enables you to search in your particular state for the laws that specifically apply to you and your housing situation.

The Mortgage

If you are simultaneously juggling a mortgage with an unplanned interlude of unemployment, the same general reasoning that applied to the landlord-tenant applies to the lender-borrower. The difference is that you should contact your mortgage lender and not your landlord. When you come up short in making a mortgage payment, it is always recommended that you place a call—post haste—to your lender and explain your tenuous position. Lay it on the line that you are experiencing financial jelly legs but expect to be back on solid ground shortly.

Foremost, find out—if you don't already know—if involuntary unemployment insurance (IUI) covers your mortgage. This type of insurance is sometimes part and parcel of mortgage agreements and will pay principal, interest, taxes, and insurance up to $2,000 a month for six months in the event of the borrower's job loss.

As the mortgage crisis of recent times reveals in one case after another, lenders will work with borrowers in many instances. They'll lend a helping hand, as it were, before initiating foreclosure proceedings. And this isn't because they are a caring bunch of Peace Corps volunteer types; it's because they frequently lose money when foreclosing on properties. From start to finish, foreclosure is an expensive and elongated legal procedure, and, on top of everything else, the repossessed properties are not always easy sells. Many, in fact, are sold at prices that don't come near recouping the original loan principals.

So, yes, it's not uncommon for banks and other mortgage lenders to work with distressed borrowers who are temporarily unemployed. Lenders take into account past incomes and loan payment histories, as well as overall expenses and spending habits. If you are a pretty responsible individual, which you no doubt are since you're reading this book, it's not inconceivable that your lender might suspend payment due for several months, while offering you a subsequent repayment plan that would enable you to slowly but surely right the course of your wayward ship. One scenario is that, upon getting a job, you begin paying the loan at its original monthly payment, with the past due amount re-amortized to the current principal. In other words, if you missed six months of payments due to unemployment, you wouldn't have to pay back that amount plus interest and late fees; instead, it would be added to the loan principal and payable over the lifetime of the loan. Again, and this bears repeating, lenders don't want to see you sitting on a rocking chair at the curbside of your *former* residence.

An Unemployment Checklist
Upon Getting the News

+ Don't push the panic button.
+ Make certain that you take everything that is rightfully yours away from the job you're departing, looking into possible accrued vacation time, overtime, back pay, and sick pay.
+ If you've been offered a severance package, go over the particulars with a fine-toothed comb. If you deem it in your best interest, make a counteroffer to the original deal. You have that right. This is not the time to be bashful.
+ If you are parting on amicable terms, seek positive references from your soon-to-be ex-employer. This will enhance both the prospects and the rapidity of you locating a satisfying new job.
+ If possible, keep your health coverage in place. Foremost, see if your employer can keep you on the company plan for the fleeting period of time that you'll be looking for another job. If this isn't in the cards, explore options such as COBRA or joining your spouse's group insurance plan. If your life profile doesn't jibe with the aforementioned possibilities, consider a form of temporary health insurance to serve as a bridge until you find regular work.

Your First Week of Being a Jobless Statistic

+ If you qualify, apply for unemployment benefits.

+ Assess your overall financial situation, beginning with what you have in ready savings to tide you over during your joblessness. Compare your assets with your expenses. Put it all down on paper.

+ Appraise your housing situation and whether it's feasible to continue living at your present address without a source of regular income. If it's not, consider alternatives, including taking in a roommate, subletting, selling (if it's a mortgaged piece of property), or relocating altogether.

+ Reduce your expenses, such as cell phone minutes, size of your cable television package, and other nonessentials in your life.

+ Shop wisely in all areas, from food to clothing, seeking out bargains and sales.

+ Keep credit card use to a bare minimum.

+ Update and refine your résumé.

+ Prepare a job search plan, starting with the placement of your résumé in as many productive places as possible.

Your First Month Without a Job

+ Put your network of former business associates, as well as family, friends, and neighbors, to work for you. That is, make all of these people your eyes and ears for potential jobs and career opportunities.

+ Attend job fairs, which are ideal places to add to your network, if not find an actual job or career path.

+ Utilize the Internet in your overall job search by placing your résumé on such websites as Monster.com, HotJobs.Yahoo.com, and CareerBuilder.com.

+ To cast your net far and wide, register with employment agencies and job recruiters.

+ Take a part-time job, or find moneymaking asides, to reduce any financial gaps. But don't permit these efforts to sidetrack your permanent job or career search.

+ Use your non-work schedule and free hours to accomplish things you couldn't get done while laboring in a full-time job, including household projects like cleaning, painting, and repairing.

+ Allow yourself as many leisure activities as possible to minimize anxiety and stress. Feel free to have fun during your joblessness.

+ Keep yourself fit by paying close attention to proper diet and exercise. This period of your life is not the time to overeat or imbibe excessive amounts of the grape.

Months into Your Joblessness

+ If necessary, trim more fat from your expenses. Look now more closely at what you deem the necessities, and see if you can't find savings here, such as selling your expensive car and getting a cheaper one.

+ If you fall behind in your rent or mortgage payments, communicate with your landlord or lender. Rather than ignore phone calls and past due notices, which can only lead to problems down the road, it pays to lay it on the line.

+ If prospects look dim in your chosen career field, contemplate a possible change into a more favorable employment environment.

+ Contemplate a change in geographic locations to where the job climate is more hospitable to what you can offer an employer, and perhaps where the cost of living is more to your liking.

✦ If you need an infusion of cash to bridge any financial chasms, put the bite on your relatives or close friends first. Explore all options before sending your credit card balances through the roof or taking out any payday-style loans. Put lower interest rates and more equitable terms ahead of your pride.

✦ Remain calm and collected as always, realizing that your luck will shortly turn.

Cashing In

In spite of the cost of living, it's still popular.

—Kathleen Norris

During the 1970s, the federal government's measure of inflationary pressures in the economy went through the proverbial roof. Inflation repartee—i.e., chitchat about rising prices—resounded from the barroom to the beauty parlor to the supermarket checkout line. Campaigning for the White House in 1980, Ronald Reagan converted the high cost of living into a winning political issue. Adding together the skyrocketing inflation and unemployment indices, the candidate even coined a new term: the *misery index.*

Since those pricey times of more than a quarter of a century ago, the government's inflation figures have precipitously fallen, but we know better than to take solace from such bureaucratic calculations. Today, the cost of living in the U.S. is higher than it's ever been. There's no getting around what's plainly staring in our faces and taking direct aim at our pocketbooks.

Prices are rising—and rising some more—on everything from a gallon of milk to a gallon of gasoline; from the electric bill to the cable television bill; from meals in restaurants to meals at the kitchen table. And to add even more costly fuel to these high-price fires that are raging in every quarter of our lives, we are clearly getting *less for more* in instance after instance. That is, a can of coffee grows in price and shrinks in size; insurance premiums cost more and cover less; highway tolls rise and the roads we drive on fall into further disrepair. So, you're no doubt wondering what you can do to successfully wage war against what is clearly a double whammy: rising prices and decreasing value. Exactly what strategies can you employ—particularly when you are out of a job and stretching every penny—to accomplish this not inconsiderable mission?

Making Do With Less: It's Not Only Doable but Uplifting

Notwithstanding the sea of negative trends working against you in the saving-money department, there are some positive realities out there that can nobly assist you in offsetting the high cost of living. It is often just a matter of knowing where to look for savings, being proactive in seeking out the best bangs for your buck, and taking advantage of what's yours for the asking.

EXERCISE:

Where Can You Save?

To get the savings ball rolling, it's imperative that you, foremost, identify where you spend your money. Once you've got a handle on precisely where your dollars flow, you can ascertain the specific areas, and the particulars therein, where savings can be realized. Ask yourself the following questions and put your answers on paper:

1. What are my fixed monthly expenses—my overhead for living (rent, mortgage payment, insurances, cable television premium, car payment, and so on)?

   _____

   _____

   _____

2. What is the average range of my monthly utility bills (such as gas, electric, and phone service)?

   _____

   _____

3. How much do I spend on food? Where do I purchase my groceries and household items?

   _____

   _____

4. How much do I spend on clothing? Where do I make these fashion purchases?

   _____

   _____

   _____

5. How much do I spend in traveling from point A to point B in any given month (including car maintenance and gas, mass transit, or car service)?

_____

_____

6. How much do I allocate per month on an Internet service provider and computer-related services?

_____

_____

7. How much do I pay out of pocket for medical coverage and health-related matters?

_____

_____

8. How much do I apportion per month on extracurricular activities (such as memberships in health clubs or attending sporting events)?

_____

9. To what degree do I splurge on leisure items every month (book purchases, magazine subscriptions, and so on)?

_____

_____

10. Do I have education-specific bills for my offspring?

_____

_____

_____

Obviously the width and breadth of your expenses will vary considerably based on your unique life circumstances—i.e., renting versus home ownership; married or single; children or no children; living in New York City or International Falls, Minnesota. Nevertheless, in most, if not all, of your expense categories, there are potential savings to be found.

The Big Three

The choicest plum that can be plucked from the free market tree is, in fact, *choices*. Competition on countless commercial fronts enables us to shop around for better deals and to realize savings. But all too often in life we select complacency over action. We opt to maintain the status quo. We just don't want to be bothered. And, of course, we procrastinate.

It often takes something dramatic like a stretch of unemployment to wake us up from our profligate slumber. When money becomes tight, we are confronted head-on with the absolute need to cut costs and save dollars *wherever* and *whenever* we can.

One sprawling savings arena that is unique to the twenty-first century—and one that so many of us fail to avail ourselves of—revolves around the big three: telephone, Internet, and cable television. In all too many cases, we pay three separate bills for three separate services. Yet, there are readily accessible and cheaper alternatives to this traditionally expensive route, where combining these three services into one bill via one service provider—your cable company—can save you some serious dough, not to mention afford you the convenience of making a single monthly payment instead of three.

Competition is fierce on the communications frontier these days. There's no sound reason why you should be paying a big telephone bill anymore, regardless of where you are calling, how long you are talking, and the frequency of the calls. If you have a cable television provider, you more than likely can marry your current TV package with a single-rate, unlimited telephone plan and high-speed Internet access as well.

And while still on the subject of your cable company, did you know that you can sometimes, just by asking, get a better price on a particular TV channels package? Most consumers are unaware of the vast powers careening through their fingertips. They don't realize that their cable companies are malleable corporate brutes. For example, many of us employ satellite dish networks in lieu of the behemoth cable companies to bring hundreds of TV channels into our homes. It's quite possible that your cable television provider would be receptive to your entreaties to prevent you from dropping them in favor of a competitor. Cable companies have been known, on occasion, to give their clientele a sop or two to keep them in the fold as paying customers. *But you've got to ask!*

Of Special Interest

It's worth beginning the topic to follow with this clarion call: Credit card purchases should be kept to an absolute minimum during your spell on the unemployment rolls. This period in your life is hardly a smart time to accumulate a debt load—one, in fact, that you may find insurmountable, even after you land another well-paying job.

Still, you may already be carrying credit card debt, and it's in your best interest—no pun intended—to pay particular heed to the interest. That is, you want the lowest interest rates possible on your credit card balances. Granted, you don't have to be unemployed to view the reduction of your credit card interest rates as a good thing, but right now it's a more pressing concern than ever before.

Credit card companies have been known to work with their customers on such particulars as lowering their astronomically high interest rates. After all, they compete in a bloodthirsty business environment. If you alert them that you need a break because of your current—and temporary—jobless situation, you just might find them willing to lend a helping hand. Again, not out of the goodness of their big business hearts, but because they recognize the alternative could be a default down the road.

As with your cable company and seeking a better deal, it all boils down to you contacting your creditors and requesting lower interest rates. Explain your tight circumstances and maintain communication with them. You are more apt to be treated fairly this way. The money you can save on lower interest rates could fast add up to something substantial. You have nothing to lose and everything to gain by asking for more reasonable interest rates.

Cheaper Food for Thought

Grocery-shopping savings abound. You just have to look for them. When things are coming up roses, we tend to give short shrift to genuine savings in favor of convenience. We shop at the supermarkets nearest us and not the ones with better bargains on the stuff we buy. We don't clip coupons from newspapers, or pay any attention to where the sales are and what's on sale. We buy what we want when we want it. And, too often, it's not really what we wanted after all, and it ends up in the garbage pail.

On the other hand, when you're obliged by necessity to live frugally, your eyes open wide to the myriad grocery savings at your disposal.

You purchase items on sale; you compare prices on competing brands; you take home things that you will definitely use and keep waste to an absolute minimum.

Many persons adapt to an unemployed lifestyle because they have no alternative, but then opt never to return to their previous ways, even after the money starts flowing again. Why pay more for groceries than you have to? If there are readily available coupons for the things you use, why not use them? Coupon savings can be found everywhere from in-store fliers to newspaper ads to mail promotions. Surf the Internet, too, for grocery coupons. Drop by FindSavings.com and Valpak.com—two good places to locate bargains near you.

Grocery Savings Tip List

1. Always look upon grocery shopping as a savings-a-thon.
2. Seek out and carefully peruse coupons in newspapers (particularly the Sunday editions, which are full of savings).
3. Keep your eyes peeled for sales advertised in daily newspapers, as well as in store windows.
4. Before beginning any shopping experience, pick up and scrutinize the store's flier.
5. Pay heed to coupon offers in the store aisles themselves.
6. Surf the Internet for coupons and, more specifically, check out the websites of stores where you shop.
7. Avoid shopping when your stomach is growling—i.e., when you're hungry. This is known to augur unnecessary purchases of items that look or smell appealing, but that are not budget friendly.

8.   If at all possible, shop alone. Too many cooks in this kitchen encourage buying more than you need and spending more than you want.

9.   Consider generic brands as substitutes for name brands. In many instances, the products are of equal size and quality, but significantly cheaper in price. You always pay a premium for name brands.

10.   Look closely at the sizes of what you buy. Often you are purchasing smaller items and believing you are getting a bargain.

11.   Avoid frozen meals when there are alternatives. You pay top dollar for frozen dinners when the fresher (and healthier) alternatives are available at much more budget-conscious prices.

12.   Purchase fruits and vegetables when they are in season and cheaper in price.

13.   If you know you'll use them, buy items in bulk. The economy of scale means that you save on bigger sizes, be it cereals, orange juice, pork chops, or Hot Pockets. Consider joining a wholesale price club like Costco Wholesale at Costco.com; BJ's Wholesale Club at BJS.com; or Sam's Club at SamsClub.com. If need be, team up with a family member or a friend.

14.   Check out the bottom shelves of grocery stores, which are often stocked with bargains.

15.   Bring a calculator to the grocery store to calculate savings based on sizes.

Clothes Make the Jobless Man and Woman

When your income stream temporarily goes south, it's incumbent upon you to tame your fashion budget. Just as with grocery shopping, clothes purchases can be made with savings foremost in your mind. And you can save money in this sartorial sphere without looking like a Dickensian waif.

Clothes Savings Tip Sheet

1. Always work with this rule of thumb: I'm going to wear my clothes until they wear out. That is, until they no longer do what they were meant to do.

2. Regularly inspect newspaper advertisements for clothing sales.

3. If you don't absolutely need a new article of clothing, don't buy it.

4. Conduct a thorough inventory of all your clothes and become reacquainted with garments you've long since forgotten.

5. Consider running a garage sale (if you've got a garage) or rent a table at a flea market to sell unwanted clothes.

6. Donate surplus clothes to charities and receive a tax deduction.

7. Attend garage sales, flea markets, and rummage sales to unearth clothing bargains.

8. Patronize thrift shops to find cheaply priced clothing.

9. Purchase your clothing with durability foremost in your mind.

10. Purchase versatile attire that can be worn for multiple purposes and on multiple occasions.

11. Save on expensive dry-cleaning bills by buying washable clothes.

12. Shop at end-of-season sales. For example, buy summer clothes when the summer's over.

13. Always keep your clothes clean and properly stored—i.e., neatly folded in dresser drawers and hung on hangers where appropriate.

14. Shine your own shoes rather than paying somebody to do it for you.

15. Consider repairing an expensive pair of shoes rather than purchasing a new pair.

Everything Old Is New Again

It's not always in your best interest to purchase the best that money can buy. First of all, money doesn't always buy *the best* anyway. And when you're unemployed and keeping a vigilant eye on the ebb of your cash flow, it's hardly the best time to equate high prices with high quality. Refurbished electronics, for instance—such as computers, iPods, or iPhones—are always cheaper to purchase than buying the identical products new. Refurbished merchandise is usually as *good as new*—with the same guarantees and warranties—for significantly lower prices.

When you buy a refurbished piece of merchandise, it could merely mean that the item was previously returned to the seller with the original box opened—period. In other words, refurbished merchandise typically isn't used in any way, shape, or form. It just can no longer be listed as new. More to the point, you're not buying something that's been battered around by a former owner. Refurbished products stem from customer returns, demonstration units, and overstocks. Merchandise with cosmetic imperfections is also listed as refurbished.

Little Things Mean a Lot ... of Savings

The late Senator Everett Dirksen famously quipped about the federal government's penchant for spending money. He said, "A billion here, a billion there, and pretty soon it adds up to real money." The same can be said for us. A few dollars here and a few dollars there, and eventually it adds up to real money. In virtually every aspect of your life, there are avenues to save. Beyond smart shopping to purchase groceries, clothes, and electronics, there are all sorts of money savers at your fingertips.

Quick Takes for Saving Money

What follows is an eclectic listing of everyday living particulars in which you can realize savings:

1. As an alternative to driving, walk whenever possible. You will not only save money on gasoline purchases and automobile repairs, but you'll benefit on the health frontier too.
2. Turn the lights off when you're not in a room. Why pay the electric company a penny more than you have to?
3. Get a library card and borrow books instead of purchasing them outright (present reading material excepted).
4. Save a few dollars on movie rentals by borrowing DVDs from libraries.

5. Read periodicals in libraries and on the Internet rather than maintaining expensive subscriptions.

6. Read newspapers online to save on daily newspaper purchases.

7. Consider shopping around for banking services without fees. Why pay, for example, checking account fees when you've got free checking account options?

8. Jettison expensive and unhealthy habits, such as smoking.

9. Eat in rather than out and save some big bucks.

10. If you must drive, consider not running the air conditioner when possible, which will give you better gas mileage.

11. Clean any accumulated dust out from under your refrigerator for better efficiency.

12. Get your hair cut at barber schools—they're cheaper alternatives for sure.

13. Use old shopping bags for your refuse instead of purchasing expensive garbage bags.

14. Employ draft dodgers at doorways and insulate your windows. You'll save on fuel bills this way.

15. Put your talents to work for you by making gifts for friends and relatives rather than buying expensive stuff in stores.

Unemployment Benefit #4

For the moment anyway, you can reduce the magnitude of your carbon footprint by scaling back your gas emissions, automobile and otherwise.

There's No Such Thing as a Free Lunch (Or Is There?)

Speaking in rather broad economic terms, Nobel Prize–winning economist Milton Friedman once remarked, "There's no such thing as a free lunch." But Mr. Friedman probably never unleashed a Web search on *freebies*. Wow, you'll be surprised at the many sites devoted to just this subject matter! If you are willing to look around and sample, and then sample some more, you can enjoy a free lunch or two or three.

The bottom line is that there is a cornucopia of freebies floating around in both actual reality and in the virtual ether as well. For starters, check out these websites: SmartWebBy.com, TheFreeSite.com, AbsolutelyFreebies.com, TotallyFreeStuff.com, FreeFlys.com, and TheFreeGuide.com.

In addition to the aforementioned freebie sites, which often link you directly to the manufacturing companies, there are also oodles of coupon-themed Web portals full of free offers. Businesses consistently chum for potential customers by furnishing them with free samples of their products. New items, in particular, are regularly given away in trial sizes.

Cutting across a wide spectrum of goods and services, too, there's plenty going on in the freebie arena. Some free stuff is handed to you in person; other freebies manifest themselves as redeemable coupons. It all redounds to you paying careful attention to what's going on in places ranging from the supermarket to the home center to the pet food and supply retailer. Look for product samplers and demonstrators. And comb the Internet with unrestrained abandon. There are untold testimonials from freebie enthusiasts who claim they never pay a cent for things like shampoos and soaps, for example, because there are always coupons for complimentary samples of such products.

To add even more muscle to your Internet hunt for free things, visit CouponCabin.com, Wow-Coupons.com, and CheapUncle.com. You'll unearth both savings and freebies in an eclectic swath of places, including Amazon.com, Weight Watchers, Marriott Hotels, Target, American Airlines, Dell, Wal-Mart, Staples, Circuit City, and many, many more. Seek and you shall find something for nothing, or next to nothing. And if you become an armed and ready freebie hunter during your jobless stint, you may never want to return to your old squandering ways.

Just one note of caution here: Beware of scammers. By definition a freebie's got to be free. You shouldn't be paying anybody anything to get something for *free*. If it sounds too good to be true, it is too good to be true. And don't be too quick to pay shipping and handling charges on freebies. Why send somebody $4.95 postage for a *free* bottle of shampoo? Also, make it your mission to hunt for freebies. You don't want to be the hunted. Hit the spam button and be done with anything unsolicited that finds you by e-mail.

Unemployment Benefit #5

You no longer have any colleagues who can put the bite on you for a short-term lunch loan.

Map Quest for the Unemployed: Bridges to Somewhere

While you are pursuing the right and proper job that'll simultaneously fulfill your career objectives and fill your pockets again, there are many quarters to forage in that offer temporary work, flexible hours, and pleasing part-time incomes. There is work that you can do that will not interfere with your broader job search, and that will supply you with some much appreciated greenbacks.

As an income-generating alternative to assuming a part-time job, there are also untold moneymaking possibilities that you can initiate from the comforts of home. You can be your own boss by manufacturing and selling merchandise that people want, or you can offer them coveted services. What follows is an intriguing sampling of diverse opportunities for you to mull over. We'll run the gamut here from the very broad (retail jobs) to highly specific (dog-walking) to uniquely creative (manufacturing pin-back buttons). In the big picture, this brief survey reveals that the sky is, in fact, the limit. Based on your family situation, location, special skills, and immediate financial needs, there truly are income prospects tailor-made for you.

Retail Jobs

If your circumstances necessitate a part-time job to help pay the bills while you hunt for a full-time position, you can very likely find a position in the retail slice of the economy. The reality is that this cosmic commercial sector has an insatiable appetite for responsible people to perform a whole host of jobs. Retailers are perpetually hiring. And courtesy of their never-ending needs to fill all kinds of slots in all kinds of places at all kinds of hours, you can, in many instances, locate part-time work that both complements your schedule and doesn't torpedo your enduring quest to land the real deal.

Retailers in a variety of industries are searching for able bodies to take on jobs ranging far and wide from cashiers to customer service representatives to in-store managers. Retailers regularly require help to perform in such areas as inventory, buying, sales, stock, administration, order picking and processing, loss prevention, finance—you name it. To get a healthy idea of the width and breadth of available retail work, as well as what the jobs are paying, scope out WorkInRetail.com and CraigsList.org. Both websites enable you to sift through the current help wanted ads in your particular neck of the woods. Among the hundreds of retailers that seek help online are Cingular, Foot Locker, Sears, JP Morgan Chase, IKEA, Sprint, Target, Home Depot, Toys-R-Us, and Best Buy.

Product Sampling and Demonstrating

To get a little more specific here, let's look at an ideal kind of job for an unemployed soul like you. As you meander through the aisles of supermarkets, department stores, and pet food and supply retailers—to name just a few spots—you will often times encounter men and women in the guise of product samplers and demonstrators. Samplers dispense freebies of merchandise to shoppers. Depending on the particular setting, the sample could be a tasty sliver of cheese, a tube of toothpaste, dog biscuits for Fido and Rover—you name it. Demonstrators, on the other hand, show the purchasing public how things work—literally—everything from fruit and vegetable juicers to power drills to clumping cat litters. These kinds of in-store product sampling and demonstrating moments are renowned for boosting sales on the participating merchandise.

What the average consumer is blissfully unaware of is that the individuals employed in the aforementioned roles of samplers and demonstrators are very often hired to do just that—as needed. In other words, the fellow who hands you that curiously ridged potato chip while standing behind a table in the supermarket is most probably there for a contracted period of time and not on the permanent payroll of either the potato chip company or the supermarket. Ditto the lady in the department store who sprays your wrist with a fragrant brand of perfume. More than likely, she is laboring as a freelance sales rep and earning a pleasing part-time income in the process.

Do you have what it takes for this kind of work?

To do in-store sampling or demonstrating of products at retailers (and elsewhere), you must first be ready, willing, and able to assume center stage. These kinds of jobs require that you interact with real people. As a product sampler or demonstrator, you meet and greet the consuming multitudes. In other words, this is not work for shy and retiring types. If your significant other is a laptop, there is other, more suitable part-time work for you. If, however, you are personable and articulate, you are a viable candidate for any number of these positions.

That said, when you are hired to appear at a retailer or another business venue, you are expected to both look and behave professionally. You can't show up for work resembling the Geico cavemen. Dress requirements are very often a white blouse or shirt, black pants, and black shoes. An overall presentable appearance, genial nature, and proper preparation for the specific job at hand are the three keys that can open doors for you in product sampling and demonstrating. Companies desperately need well-mannered, sociable, and reliable persons to represent them and their products. If you meet these criteria, you are a valuable human resource in many businesses' green eyes.

Where do you find these opportunities?

Sampling and demonstrating positions are available via a wide assortment of companies. The products and services that are promoted through these methods are numerous and diverse. For openers, inquire with the managers at the locations where you encounter samplers and demonstrators plying their trade—from supermarkets to department stores to pet food and supply retailers to home centers to shopping malls. Typically, they can explain to you what these jobs entail, as well as point you to open positions and specific companies that are hiring samplers and demonstrators.

In addition, there are businesses that link up interested and qualified parties with sampling and demonstrating sales jobs. Visit All-Ways In-Store at AWInStore.com. This outfit has a perpetual dragnet out for prospective samplers and demonstrators. It works with companies in all areas of commerce that utilize them.

More often than not, sampling and demonstrating work occurs on weekends. Retailers attract the most shoppers on weekends and, logically, businesses want to promote their products via samplers and demonstrators when they can tap into the deepest customer reservoirs. Fortunately, weekends just happen to be when most people are free to take on extra jobs. These jobs are ideal vehicles for the unemployed to drive away in. You can earn many welcome dollars, while not interfering with your permanent job search during the work week.

What are the income possibilities?

Product sampling and demonstrating jobs generally pay in the range of $8 to more than $15 per hour. The more experience you accrue in these entrepreneurial fields of green, the greater your worth will be to employers. It's no stretch to say that many persons in these roles earn $80 to $120 a day.

Cooking Jobs and Culinary Careers

In the retail and service sectors of the economy—fertile ground for part-time jobs—one particular area is flaming hot. A very lush and diverse job frontier exists in the wild and woolly culinary sphere. And the proof is in the pilaf. Positions for chefs, cooks, and food preparation workers are plentiful and promise to be in great demand tomorrow and the tomorrow after that. Enrollment in cooking schools all across America is also at an all-time high.

Interestingly, the surging popularity of culinary-themed TV shows has generated a star-like aura around chefs and what they do. These kitchen magicians are perceived as both artists and celebrities. And, the truth be told, a heaping helping of men and women hunger for just this kind of notoriety and view a cooking aptitude as their meal ticket, so to speak, and perhaps a great deal more than that.

Do you have what it takes for this kind of work?

The key ingredient required to convert cooking acumen into a paying part-time job or, in fact, a lifelong career is your capacity to enter a kitchen with a positive attitude and exit at the end of the day with an eagerness to return for another go around. If you already have a penchant for cooking—or desire to acquire one—you might consider enrolling in a culinary curriculum. Upon graduation from a respected cooking school, your exceptional know-how will be coveted by a wide array of employers in a wide array of places. Even if you opt not to go to cooking school, there are many positions in this employment bailiwick that call for no diploma or special coursework, but only your willingness to learn as you go.

Before jumping into the frying pan, as it were, the overriding question that you must satisfactorily answer is whether or not you want to labor in a kitchen, be it in a restaurant, hotel, school, hospital, or any number of other hotspots. Keep in mind that in the culinary world the expression, "If you can't stand the heat, get out of the kitchen," assumes a higher and very literal meaning. In other words, kitchen work is ordinarily fast-paced and pretty darn arduous. And, alas, in all too many instances the pay is not commensurate with the energy expended. Nevertheless, an awful lot of people are warmed by the heat of the kitchen and thrive in its unique brand of sweat and toil.

Where do you find these opportunities?

If you are primarily interested in additional income or part-time work as a cook or related job in a kitchen, peruse newspaper help wanted ads. The bottom line is that you don't need any special training to work in many restaurants and diners—most notably in the fast-food field. There are open positions in commercial eateries and institutional kitchens everywhere because they employ transitory workforces—waves of men and women who come and go and come and go again. Indeed, the culinary employment pie is remarkably fluid and flexible. Since the need for pairs of capable hands is so broad and constant, kitchens employ many people on a part-time basis, as well as offering flexible scheduling to suit individual needs. They are very hospitable places for unemployed persons looking for temporary sources of income.

On the other hand, if you are contemplating a career in the culinary business, there are many valuable websites in the virtual ether that can help you attain your goals and realize your dreams. These Internet portals will, among many things, inform you where the cooking schools are and where the cooking jobs are after graduation. They are full of resources. For starters, visit CookingSchools.com, Culinary-School-Finder.com, and AllCulinarySchools.com. Keep in mind that many culinary schools are costly. In other words, their tuition tabs could burn you worse than the hot oil you'll be working with. Nevertheless, there are a variety of educational avenues in this field. If a hefty tuition bill is beyond your means at the moment, carefully comb community college curriculums. Believe it or not, there are opportunities aplenty in the cooking discipline at many of these institutions of fine learning, and the costs are often a few hundred dollars—not $5,000 to $10,000 or more, which some of the more prestigious cooking schools charge.

Since the human species has got to eat to survive, you can always count on open cooking and culinary-related jobs. Positions in this vast and varied realm run a wide gamut from chefs to sous chefs ("under" chefs) to line cooks (assistant cooks) to food preparers of all stripes to short-order cooks to fast-food cooks. And the locations that require cooking help also cut across a wide swath from five-star restaurants to tourist trap eateries to greasy spoons to hospitals to schools to luxury cruise ships. Even many grocery stores and specialty food stores hire cooks, as they sell more and more ready-to-serve meals these days.

What are the income possibilities?

If there's a downside to the cornucopia of culinary work out there, it's definitely the pay scale. Unless you are in a key kitchen position, wages are generally in the range of $8 to $12 per hour, even in some very upscale restaurants. If, however, you possess cooking skills, your services will be highly desired. That is, you can move from kitchen to kitchen, pad your résumé, and earn bigger and bigger paychecks over time.

Unemployment Benefit #6

Instead of purchasing a cup of coffee and a bagel from a harried street vendor in front of your workplace, you can leisurely sip your java and munch on a plate of bacon and eggs at your favorite greasy spoon.

Manufacture Something

During your jobless stint, you might consider manufacturing a product that you can sell to others for a profit. Let's explore just one of the *many* possibilities at your disposal: the simple pin-back button. Yes, it's long been a tradition of ours to make a statement, or to reveal something about ourselves, by affixing pin-back buttons to our jackets, shirts, and bags. Whether the buttons trumpet our backing of a preferred political candidate, love for a particular breed of dog, devotion to a favorite sports team, or support for any number of causes, they speak volumes.

So, it should come as no surprise to you that button manufacturing is a very profitable business sphere. It's also an ideal avenue to venture down for supplementary income. That is, you can be a pin-back button maker and realize a considerable profit by churning them out in your spare time.

Do you have what it takes for this kind of work?

To commence manufacturing pin-backs, all that is needed is a button machine and the requisite button parts. When you acquire these accoutrements, you are in essence open for business. And, should you want to start slow and test the market, beginner button paraphernalia can be had on the cheap. A rudimentary, hand-held button machine can be purchased for under $50. Of course, you have the option to invest significant dollars in much more sophisticated equipment. Durable button machines capable of mass-producing pin-backs cost a couple of hundred dollars and up. Your decision in this investment arena depends entirely on what you have to put into your button business and how far you want to take your enterprise.

There are numerous button machine and related equipment manufacturers to scope out and compare both products and prices, including Badge-A-Minit at Badge-A-Minit.com (1-800-776-3633), Dr. Don's Buttons at ButtonsOnline.com (1-800-243-8293), American Button Machines at AmericanButtonMachines.com (972-985-5074), and Badge Parts at BadgeParts.com (1-800-776-3633). Many of these companies also offer button-design CDs that enable you to generate your very own artwork on the computer. If you'd rather not—or cannot—do it yourself, some of these outfits have in-house art departments to create the necessary designs for you.

To make money in the button business, you needn't even purchase a stitch of equipment. You can have a button manufacturer custom-make the pin-backs for you. You harvest the orders and farm out the manufacturing to a company that makes buttons. You can provide the design you want pictured on the buttons—or have everything from A to Z done for you. You can also take your own ideas for buttons, have them made by somebody else, and retail them for very nice profits at all kinds of venues.

Where do you find these opportunities?

Attend flea markets, fairs, rallies, and community events to peddle your buttons. You can sell general interest pin-backs on eBay. You can take orders from local schools, political campaigns, and all kinds of clubs and associations. While perusing button manufacturers' websites, you'll encounter oodles of ideas on where you can unearth customers for buttons. When it comes to finding pin-back button business, there are few restricted areas.

What are the income possibilities?

Look at it this way: If it costs you $0.40 or $0.50 to produce a product that you can retail for $1.50 or $2.00, you can realize a nice return. There is ample room to wholesale buttons and make a fair profit as well.

If you have any doubt about the popularity of pin-back buttons and related *expression* products—T-shirts, bumper stickers, refrigerator magnets, etc.—check out CafePress.com. You might want to sell your ideas here, and perhaps even add to their unemployment line, which features various slogans on buttons, T-shirts, bumper stickers, and more, such as: "Streamline Business: Outsource the CEOs"; "If You Think the System is Working, Ask Someone Who Isn't"; "I Do Many Things Well, None of Which Generates an Income"; "Unemployment Runs in My Family"; "Will Work for Cold Hard Cash"; "Occupationally Challenged"; "Who Moved My Cheese to India?"; "I'm Fired"; and "Unemployment Made in the U.S.A., Assembled in China."

Crank Up the At-Home Assembly Line

Pin-back button production is merely one example of the many moneymaking possibilities available to you. We'll call this the at-home manufacturing sector. What follows is a list of part-time income ideas that just might jibe with your unique talents or be of particular interest to you in your present jobless incarnation. From your home base, you can manufacture:

1. Candles
2. Soaps
3. Greeting cards
4. Engraved plaques
5. Jams and jellies
6. Cakes and pies
7. Dog biscuits
8. Cat and dog playthings
9. Decorative wreaths
10. Candies and chocolates
11. Jewelry
12. Children's clothing
13. Christmas ornaments
14. Special crafts
15. Unique paintings

Sell the fruits of your labor at craft fairs and flea markets. Call on appropriate retailers. Peddle them on eBay or a website of your own. There are many avenues for you to sell what you make. And the beauty is that you can do it all in your spare time and not sidetrack your traditional job search. Of course, you just might discover that a full-time business of manufacturing and selling your own merchandise is not pie-in-the-sky.

Dog-Walking

Once upon a time, you asked a neighbor, or a neighbor's kid, to walk your dog when life's myriad demands spirited you away for extended periods of time. In many instances, you requested that your four-legged friend hold it all in until you returned home from wherever life's responsibilities took you.

Nowadays, increasing numbers of the two-legged among the dog-owning populace—more commonly known as *pet parents*—couldn't conceive of asking their best friends to resist nature's call for eight or more hours at a time. And, the truth be told, there are fewer and fewer reliable neighbors around to assume the task of walking your canine buddy. The by-product of this new reality is an industry within the burgeoning broader trade known as pet care. For lack of a more elevating description, we're talking about dog-walking. That is, you walk people's pooches for specified periods at agreed-upon times of the day and get compensated for providing said services.

Do you have what it takes for this kind of work?

There are no laws that mandate any particular credentials or accreditation to walk dogs. However, there are local by-laws regarding what you must do with their waste products. So, to condense this answer a bit, it behooves you to know what you're getting into here. It's also important that you have more than a modicum of canine knowledge. Being a dog parent yourself, and liking the species a whole lot, can only benefit you in this entrepreneurial endeavor.

In fact, many professional dog-walking outfits are insured and bonded. If you want to do this kind of work in a grand way—maybe even make it your career—you've got to wade through the minutiae. After all, dog-walking and its more expansive cousin, pet-sitting, require your entrance into clientele's homes when they aren't on the premises. As you can see, there's a considerable matter of trust here, particularly when you add to this equation the fact that you are caring for bona fide members of people's families—not just house pets.

Where do you find these opportunities?

If you're merely looking for a little extra income while serving your sentence as a jobless statistic, just pass the word around that you're open for business. Word of mouth and a dependable reputation bring you customers in this field. If you want to take this part-time income thing even further, pass out fliers and run ads in local papers.

As an alternative to starting from scratch, you could seek part-time work at already established dog-walking and pet-sitting outfits. Many of these businesses require extra hands to build up their client bases. And your hands are as a good as any. You might want to check out the National Association of Professional Pet Sitters (NAPPS) at PetSitters. org, which will furnish you with a fair share of information on this entrepreneurial undertaking, including where you can purchase appropriate insurance.

What are the income possibilities?

Dog-walking rates range from $15 to $25—and sometimes more than that—per half hour. So much depends on what you do with that half hour and where you go. If you call a big city home, you've probably seen people walking five or more dogs at once. What you've witnessed is more likely a dog-walking service than an owner of a canine menagerie. To reiterate: This business requires that you know what you're doing and are responsible all across the board. If, for instance, you're walking multiple dogs at the same time, you've got to know the dogs you're taking out for a stroll. Not every canine would countenance walking in the company of complete strangers, even if they are of the same species.

Service with a Smile

Dog-walking is a service. And there are numerous services that you could provide the needy multitudes while in a state of unemployment. For instance, when Old Man Winter's snows come blowing in, there are lots of folks who desperately need a pair of hands to shovel it all away. And, guess what, even the neighborhood kids are pulling in $25 to $50 and more for clearing snow from driveways and sidewalks. In the big picture, there are countless services you can supply to others that they'll happily pay you for.

Are you are handy with a paintbrush or with household repairs? Why not make it known that you are available for jobs? Professional housepainters charge $1.50 to $2.00 per square foot. If you are all thumbs and can't hammer a nail in straight—don't fret! You're still a valuable commodity. Put the word out that you're reliable, trustworthy, and at the ready to housesit or babysit. Demand always exceeds supply for caretakers of both children and the elderly. Does $15 an hour and better sound like something you can use? Talk with family, friends, and neighbors who always seem to know people who need people. Look too in classified ads in local newspapers, as well as on bulletin boards in libraries and at supermarkets. A book worth checking out in this quirky employment area is *Odd Jobs* by Abigail Gehring.

Unemployment Benefit #7

Courtesy of not having one at the present time, you are fully liberated from the perpetual fretting over the monies taken out of your paycheck.

Swimming in the Rewarding Surf of eBay

Believe it or not, there was once a world without eBay. It was a cold, cruel place that didn't permit us to rummage through our closet and earn a nice piece of change from its superfluous contents. It was a world that asked us to go to some rather extraordinary lengths—like running classified ads in newspapers—to sell everything from unwanted furniture to obsolete electronics to invaluable coin and stamp collections. As fate would have it, you do not reside on the pre-eBay planet just described. You've got immediate access to a thriving international marketplace that connects oodles of eager sellers with insatiably hungry buyers on just about every kind of item imaginable—and that's no exaggeration.

What you can sell on eBay knows few boundaries. You can place on auction—or peddle outright via Buy It Now—coveted collectibles, articles of clothing, computer parts, household items, sporting goods, books—you name it. Even automobiles and real estate are now readily available on this online auction giant. For our unique purposes here, let's just say that the inviting waters of eBay are a jobless individual's godsend.

eBay Disclaimer

Before venturing any further in this lush field, it's important for you to realize that it's highly unlikely that you'll convert your overstuffed closets, or the contents of your garage, into a fortune that would inspire a "Talk to Chuck" moment. Nor is it probable that selling stuff on eBay will become your next full-time job (even though thousands of men and women make their livings doing just that). Maybe you have a Honus Wagner T-206 baseball card lying around in mint condition—then all bets are off. (This small sliver of cardboard is considered the "Mona Lisa of baseball cards" and recently sold at auction for more than $2 million!)

Working with the assumption that you don't have one of those vintage tobacco baseball cards on hand, you would be better served to approach eBay transacting as a surefire way to put some welcome dollars into your increasingly forlorn bank account. You can, in fact, sell stuff that you don't necessarily need or want anymore. There are probably persons interested in acquiring these very things—and they're surfing the waves of eBay right now.

In a nutshell, it's precisely this marriage of sellers with buyers that makes eBay tick. And it's actually a match made in heaven while you're sans a paying job. On top of everything else, selling things on eBay is a whole lot of fun. If you've never participated in the fast and furious eBay buying and selling arena, you don't know what you've been missing. The natural high in witnessing something you've got at auction going up and up in price as bidders compete for it is unrivaled. In real time, you can keep a watchful eye on your auctions as they unfold to their—hopefully—lucrative conclusions.

eBay Basics

Selling on eBay is truly a piece of cake. If you're not already part of the eBay fraternity, you will have to first register with the online conglomerate at eBay.com. This is a rather straightforward process that you can accomplish in a matter of minutes. If you have access to a computer, can get on the Internet, and have the wherewithal to type with one finger or more, you are poised on the precipice of earning some cash—or, perhaps, a whole lot of the green stuff. To merely place bids or purchase things on eBay, you needn't provide any detailed personal information. However, to sell merchandise, you'll have to furnish credit card information or make a single payment directly to eBay to keep on account.

Yes, eBay is a profit-making entity and charges fees for its myriad services. You are billed monthly for whatever fees you accrue during that time frame. The company bills your credit card or debits money that you have on account with them. These charges emanate from non-refundable listing fees for each item that you place on auction. In addition, you part with a small percentage of the final sale of every piece of merchandise that sells. But we're talking about relatively small amounts, always less than 10 percent of the winning bids, and significantly below that figure as the dollar amounts reach higher and higher stratospheres. In other words, you keep the preponderance of the final sales.

eBay Selling ABCs

The eBay selling process is elementary. Here's what you do:

1. Register with eBay as a seller. You select a user ID and password.

2. Unearth items that you both want to sell and that you also believe will sell. Comb through the eBay site to ascertain exactly what's selling and what's getting bids.

3. Photograph the merchandise that you plan to put on auction. Since you can upload the photographs directly from your hard drive to eBay, a digital camera works best here. If you don't own a digital camera—and cannot borrow one from somebody who does—an old-fashioned camera will suffice. However, by going this route, you will have to scan the physical pictures, save them on your hard drive, and then upload them to eBay.

4. Now comes the moment of truth when you list your item and cast your fate to the wind, as it were. You begin by clicking on the Sell link on the eBay site. Upon entering your user ID and password, you are guided through a process that asks you to create a title heading, upload photos, set a starting bid amount (or Buy It Now price), establish the duration of the auction (three days, five days, seven days, or ten days), furnish a complete description of your item for sale, fix postage charges, and determine the methods of payments that you will accept. During this listing procedure, you also select a category (or multiple categories) where your item will be featured. This is very important for obvious reasons. You don't want to auction off a camcorder and have it appear in the Music category alongside multiple thousands of CDs. You wouldn't want to sell an MP3 player and list it under Sporting Goods, where people are searching for things like golf clubs and tennis rackets. The bottom line is that you want to maximize your sales by getting as many people as possible to visit and peruse your listing page.

5. When you've completed all the requisite administrative work, it's time—after a careful review of the information you've furnished, which you are afforded as the penultimate step—to click List My Item. Shortly thereafter, your piece of merchandise is on the auction block for the entire world to see.

eBay Tips

While selling merchandise on eBay is not rocket science—in fact, it's so easy a caveman could do it—it is, nevertheless, a business contract. That is, at the end of the day—or, in this instance, the end of your auctions—you've got to properly package and timely ship the goods to real live human beings who have paid you real live dollars.

Some folks are under the misapprehension that eBay selling amounts to an autopilot business. After all, everything transpires online and you never physically see a flesh-and-blood person, and rarely, if ever, speak with one. But the reality is that you may have to answer e-mail queries from interested parties throughout your active auctions. You may also have to deal with disgruntled customers every now and again, who, rightly or wrongly, feel that they've gotten the shaft from you. This is why you must enter the eBay selling arena with your professional hat atop your head. Maintain professionalism throughout the entire selling process by:

✦ Thoroughly and accurately describing your items on auction, detailing any and all imperfections.

✦ Honestly responding to any questions that come your way during an auction.

✦ Shipping your merchandise without delay and packaged well.

✦ Making amends to unhappy buyers, even if you feel you are in the right.

✦ Leaving positive feedback for buyers who comply with the eBay contract of promptly paying for what they win or purchase outright.

eBay Feedback

Sellers on eBay live and die by their feedback ratings. Since there is no other way to assess the integrity (or lack thereof) of eBay members, feedback assumes a monumental role in separating the good guys and gals from the rotten eggs.

As an eBay seller, you want satisfied customers to leave you positive feedback. As you begin to accumulate testimonials from winning bidders, more and more prospective buyers will visit your auctions and consider bidding on what you have to sell. Positive feedback will not only attract more potential customers to your items, but their willingness to bid—and bid higher still—will be greater. People don't like getting ripped off, or outright scammed, and appreciate a true professional with a track record of upright dealings. So, even if you're merely emptying out your closets and selling the contents on eBay, look upon what you're doing as a business, because that's exactly what it is. Also, don't view your eBay transacting as merely a jobless aside. Consider it part of your life in perpetuity. You can always use a few extra dollars. And if you've got things that you can sell on eBay in the future, why not convert them into added income—even if you're rolling in the dough?

What to Sell on eBay

Since its rather inconspicuous inception in 1995, eBay has evolved into an international phenomenon. In other words, everybody and their grandparents know about the global auction leviathan and are peddling their wares on eBay, including brick-and-mortar businesses. What all this means is that the competition gets pretty stiff sometimes.

When eBay first opened its virtual doors, it was a genuine bonanza for many sellers, particularly collectors. Rare, hard-to-locate items consistently brought in big bucks. Today, in many instances, those once-upon-a-time rare items are decidedly less so. When the whole wide world is cleaning out their closets and garages, it stands to reason that a scarce Hummel figurine will be more readily available, as will a vintage Topps baseball card, and that certain piece of Depression glass, too. That said, eBay is still an ideal place to sell what you have and connect with buyers looking for exactly that.

Fortunately, coupled with the increasing competition among sellers is a simultaneous upsurge in buyers, and this reality is what works in your favor. Very likely, there are countless items in your home that you can parlay into dollars. You've just got to find bidding suitors. So, just what do you have in your possession that will *sell* on eBay? Here are some broad classifications of the kind of things that consistently locate buyers on eBay:

+ **Vintage collectibles.** Even though the competition in this area is more robust than ever before, it's still the most potentially lucrative. Generally speaking, if you own any older things (pre-1980) that are deemed collectible—from baseball cards to figurines to kids' toys—you might just have a diamond or two in the rough. As with all collectible items, the better the condition, the more valuable the piece. If an original product came in a box, having that box is a real boon when it comes to maximizing final sales at auction.

+ **Consumer electronics.** This is always a productive area for selling. People are forever looking for bargains in this department. Why pay top dollar in a big-box retailer when the same piece of merchandise can be had on eBay? If you have anything from an iPod to a telephone to a car stereo to a DVD player, even if the item is previously used, you've got a potential seller on your hands. Again, new in the original box is best, but *like new* condition—particularly on high-price electronics—is the next best thing.

+ **Computer accessories.** Need we say it, computers and computer-related products are big—really big—sellers on eBay. Perhaps you have some spare parts, as it were, that you don't need. Everything from network cables to software to keyboards is sold on eBay.

+ **Cell phone accessories.** This is the twenty-first century and these are the items—along with computers—that captivate one and all across the sociological spectrum and indeed across the world.

+ **Quality fashions and clothing accessories.** If you've got unused apparel and related materials that people are interested in, you'll have no problem finding an audience of eager eBayers.

+ **Sporting, exercise, and fitness goods.** Have any quality sports and recreation-related items lying around, such as golf clubs, baseball bats, and exercise bikes? These kinds of things sell.

+ **DVDs.** If you have accumulated a library of movies, now might be a good time to sell some of them on eBay. Previously viewed

DVDs do very well in online auctions, and are a nice way for you to generate some welcome income while parting with movies you probably weren't going to watch again.

✦ **CDs.** Have you amassed a monster of a CD collection—one that far surpasses your listening needs and takes up an awful lot of space? Exactly how many of these CDs do you listen to? Place the ones that are just sitting there and collecting dust on eBay. Let's say you have fifty CDs to sell and average $5 on each one—that's $250 in your pocket. As is so often the case, it's like found money!

✦ **Cameras and photo equipment.** With technology advancing faster than a speeding bullet, perhaps you have an old camera— or related products such as lenses or filters—that somebody else might crave.

✦ **Jewelry and watches.** Your jewelry box or drawer might be running over with pieces that you'll never wear again, or that maintain some value that you'd like to cash in at this time in your life.

✦ **Hardcover books.** Just finished reading a recently released hardcover, or perhaps you received one as a gift that you have no intention of ever reading? Why not put it on eBay? Granted, you won't likely earn the cover price, or anything close to it, but five to ten dollars more in your pocket isn't chump change.

eBay Essentials

If you haven't already done so, sign up with PayPal at PayPal.com, which is an eBay company. With a verified PayPal account, you can facilitate credit card transactions on eBay, which are essential to maximizing your auction sales. In addition, your PayPal account could prove useful in areas well outside of eBay auctioneering. Many Internet businesses accept PayPal funds. Therefore, if you've got cash in your PayPal account, you can purchase things from others with the accumulated funds. When you so desire, PayPal electronically deposits funds into your bank account.

Never give short shrift to describing the various items you place on eBay. The more thorough the descriptions, the more potential bidders will come your way. For one, people search for things on eBay utilizing key words. In other words, what you put in your merchandise titles and descriptions is critical. You have nothing to gain—and everything to lose—by penning one to two line descriptions of the things you sell.

Don't shortchange yourself or overcharge your customers on shipping costs. Too high a shipping rate drives potential bidders away. Too low a shipping rate cuts into your profits. Visit your shipping alternatives to ascertain cost estimates based on package weights and geographic locations: United States Postal Service (USPS) at USPS. com; United Parcel Service (UPS) at UPS.com; and FedEx at FedEx. com.

If you'd rather not—or cannot logistically—sell things on eBay, you have the option to have somebody else do it for you. There are eBay businesses everywhere. These are outfits that will do all the work and put your stuff on eBay (if, of course, they determine that it's both sellable and worth their time and efforts). For their troubles, they'll take in the neighborhood of 30 percent of the final sales generated.

On the flip side of your having a third party peddle your goods on eBay, you could sell other people's stuff for them. And you can charge them 30 percent of what the auction brings in. Not bad. When you're unemployed, you've certainly got the time to venture down this route.

And the beauty of eBay is that there are no business hours. You can ply your trade at two o'clock in the morning or at lunchtime; it doesn't matter a whit.

How to Live on Less Than $20 a Day

When the sun rises and the rooster crows, you've been served notice to inaugurate yet another productive *and frugal* day of unemployed living. By neatly blending together all that we've gleaned thus far about unearthing savings in every imaginable corner of our lives—plus taking full advantage of coupons and freebies—we've constructed a first-of-its-kind $20 a day roadmap. Where feasible, walk the walk of these tried-and-true steps and you are guaranteed to—at the end of the day—tally up to less than $20 of expenditures:

1. For starters, let's put on the morning pot of coffee. But were you aware that yesterday's coffee grinds often have quite a bit more yield left in them? Use half of the old stuff with a half helping of fresh coffee and you'll achieve both a decent brew and savings too—a nice way to commence your pennywise day.

2. Why not eat a frugal *and healthy* breakfast along with that aromatic coffee blend? Combine thriftiness with wholesome eating whenever and wherever possible. Instead of bacon and eggs, cream cheese on bagels, pancakes, and waffles, opt for a breakfast like oatmeal. It's relatively cheap in price, easy enough to prepare, and pretty tasty when you complement it with extras like fresh fruit, almonds, or cinnamon. Consider eating a breakfast grapefruit sprinkled with some sugar. Grapefruits are quite cheap in comparison to other fruits because of their robust

dimensions—and good for you, too. Whole-grain, high fiber cereals are certainly better choices than donuts, muffins, and most breakfast bars—and, for our immediate purposes, budget friendly. Breakfast: under $1.50.

3. Get dressed for your jobless day's itinerary, emphasizing durable attire above all else. And wash your clothes *only* when they are certifiably dirty. In other words, don't throw your clothes into the hamper at the end of the day merely because it's the end of the day. Washing things less frequently adds up to genuine savings in and of itself. In addition, fewer washings and dryings significantly extend the lives of most articles of clothing.

4. Map out your scheduled destinations for the day with this frugal formula in mind: *Walk is cheap*, so walk to places within walking distance; bicycling is next best; mass transit has its place; hop in the car *only* to travel very far. Granted, for some men and women the term "within walking distance" could mean two or three miles; for others, destinations that are two or three blocks away might as well be in another time zone. In any event, cutting down on automobile travel in this era of astronomically high gas prices and car maintenance costs is a paramount money saver. Daily travel expenses: under $5.00.

5. Prepare a bag lunch. Keep eating out to an absolute minimum. Even the ubiquitous slice of pizza has skyrocketed in price due to the excessive cost of flour (and everything else, for that matter). A healthy lunch prepared by you at the start of the day saves you bona fide dollars. Even an unhealthy one prepared with love in your kitchen is a cheaper alternative than a stop at McDonald's, Subway, or even the hot dog vendor. Make your own sandwich and add a banana and a carrot to the mix. (Bananas are cheap, available year round, very portable, and full of healthy necessities like potassium, fiber, and vitamin B6. Carrots, too, fit a similar bill. However, avoid baby carrots. Buy the big ones and peel them yourself. You'll save big on the big ones.) Lunch: under $3.00.

6. Rather than purchase the morning newspapers, visit the local library and read them there (or via your computer, of course). Utilize libraries not only for reading newspapers and magazines (cut out those expensive subscriptions), but for your determined job search as well. There are *free* resources aplenty in libraries. Newspaper and periodical costs: $0.

7. Thirsty during your jobless travels? Well, no more gulping down sodas or bottled drinks—and this includes bottled water. News alert: Millions of people have imbibed run-of-the-mill tap water and have lived to tell about it! Fill up the empties of your formerly favorite bottled water with *free*—and free flowing—tap water. Carry them around with you on your adventures and misadventures from point A to point B. You will surely save nifty piece of change this way. Beverage costs: $0.

8. If you have any unhealthy habits, jobless time is the prime cold-turkey time. Be it smoking cigarettes or a related leafy plant, kick it off your daily menu. If you have a penchant for alcohol in any of its spirited incarnations, go on the wagon—at least for the time being. Bad habits are very costly. In New York City, for instance, the political sin doctors have piled up so many taxes on a pack of the poisonous pleasures that the cost is getting darn near close to the price of a movie ticket. Cold-turkey costs: $0.

9. Wherever your unemployed odyssey finds you—including all of your job search downtime—avoid going into shopping malls, or individual retailers, just to browse. Shop where you absolutely need to shop—period. Daily cost of this minor self-restraint on your part: $0.

10. For your everyday household needs, consider shopping in 99-cent stores or their parsimonious equivalents. There are lots of bargains in these joints on everything from soaps to shower curtain liners to canned soups to electrical tape. But carefully scrutinize what you're buying beyond the pleasing 99-cent price tags. There are many things for sale in these establishments that are indeed cheaply priced, but that are also cheaply manufactured—and therefore not worth even one of your precious dollars. Why, for instance, buy a bargain roll of paper towels for 99 cents when a competitive brand, at $1.69, will last you three or four times as long? Do the arithmetic!

11. If at all possible, shop for groceries in one fell swoop. That is, purchase tonight's dinner along with tomorrow's breakfast and lunch (or, better yet, several days' meals at one time). Bring with you all of your accumulated coupons and pay extra-special attention to the store's current sales. In your frugal mindset, focus on foodstuffs like beans. They are loaded with proteins, fiber, and lots of other healthy things. And, on top of that, there's so much you can do with them! Buy them dry or in ready-to-serve cans. Make soups, salads, or chili with them. Pour your favorite beans over brown rice (another cheap and healthy product), and you've got yourself a quality dinner (at under $1.50 a serving). It's a capital idea to always *think versatile* while shopping for food particulars. There are other breakfast, lunch, and dinner items that are both reasonably priced and adaptable to a variety of dishes and a variety of moments. Eggs are a supreme example.

You can eat them at all times during the day and in many manifestations. For instance, eggs with toast in the morning and eggs in omelets at suppertime. Dinner: under $4.00.

12. During your unemployed free moments, seek out free entertainment instead of costly movie admissions and other expensive leisure adventures. There are ample fun places you can go, and interesting things you can see, without parting with a thin dime. For starters, check out Free-Attractions.com for just those things. This website enables you to search by state—and individual cities in many cases—to locate entertaining places and venues that won't invade your wallet. Examples of the kinds of things featured on this site: museums, parks, concerts, parades, festivals, zoos, and much more. Your local dailies always feature information on free entertainment. Library bulletin boards are also worth looking over for cultural happenings. Entertainment costs: $0.

13. Home at night from a fast-paced day of looking for work, spending very little of your money, and having a grand old time, it's now time—after your cost-conscious but very satisfying dinner—to relax in the comforts of home. Sorry, no Pay-Per-View movies tonight. Select from the menu of what you're already paying for, which is ordinarily more than sufficient as quality entertainment and a well-earned snippet of relaxation. At-home entertainment costs: $0.

14. At any free moment during your day, try reading a book (borrowed from the library, of course). Free entertainment and free knowledge: $0.

15. Finally, hankering for an after-dinner or late-night snack, why not pop your very own kernels of popcorn? It's a very inexpensive and quite tasty snack. You can accomplish this mission on your stovetop. You need only the popping corn kernels, a large pot, and a tablespoon of oil or butter. There are also ready-to-eat bags in stores of unsalted, unbuttered, and un-the-hundred-and-one other things put in traditional popcorns. Believe it or not, when popcorn is not doctored up, it still tastes good and is considered a healthy snack. Other evening snacks that won't break the bank: carrots and celery. After-dinner snacks: under $1.00.

By plotting coordinates with this map, your day's expenses compute to well under $20. This gives you some leeway in the 99-cent store and while grocery shopping. Buy that package of chicken or even a little beef when circumstances arise. Treat yourself to ice cream every now and again. When you live frugally on a day-to-day basis, you can't help but realize savings. You won't go hungry, either. And, as the *pièce de résistance*, you'll have an abundance of fun along the way.

More Time Than You Ever Thought You'd Have!

There is never enough time to do everything,
but there is always enough time to do the most important thing.

—Brian Tracy

We've heretofore touched upon various benefits of your unemployed existence, underscoring the newfound allotments of *spare time* that come with the territory. Your daily routine—from morning stretch to nighttime yawn—has unquestionably undergone a radical metamorphosis since the loss of your job and corresponding livelihood.

What you do with the finite hours of the day is now largely in your own hands. You are no longer reading from an intricately plotted script. Remember the way things once were: You headed off to the job at a specified hour, performed a series of prescribed tasks while there, and then ventured home at another prescribed time—without fail—from Monday to Friday. And even in your leisure moments, you likely didn't deviate from the job-inspired script because you had to turn in by a certain hour. You had no choice but to wake up bright-eyed and bushy-tailed the following morning. The funny thing is that your myriad weekend activities were also planned around returning to work early on Monday. And your vacations, too, weren't they all mapped out well in advance? In other words, spontaneity didn't rule the roost during your work life; an inflexible routine did. Well, that's yesterday's news. Flexibility is your friend now. For many unemployed individuals, this degree of freedom is at once liberating and, quite understandably, a bit intimidating.

Today Should Always Be the Day

Okay, now that you're certifiably unemployed and sans a full-time job, you've got a heaping helping of free time on your plate. More specifically, you have time in front of you that's not choreographed from the cock's morning crow to the evening's lights out. But calling it *free* time is something of a misnomer. If you were past retirement age with a tidy nest egg to fall back on, healthy chunks of *actual* free time would govern your golden years. However, since you're reading this book, the odds favor that you're not sunning yourself on Florida's sandy shores, ensconced in a retirement village with an EMS vehicle at the ready, collecting monthly social security checks. The more likely scenario is that you anticipate latching on to a well-paying job, or a spanking new career path, in the very near future. Calling home a refrigerator box under the nearest highway overpass is not in your cards.

What this reality snapshot highlights is that your extreme free time—for lack of a more apt term—comes attached to a considerable price tag. That is, it behooves you to budget sizeable portions of this time to your enduring job search. In fact, make it the crowning jewel of your new routine—your jobless routine.

That said, the beauty of this brand of routine is that the daily minutiae needn't be set in stone. You can establish a general pattern of unemployed living. Commit yourself to hunting for work with all of the job safari accoutrements at your disposal, but also take full advantage of this rare moment in life when you have no firm obligations before you. Look at it this way: When the particulars of every hour of every single day are not prearranged for you, you are no longer a human wind-up doll.

Couch Potato or Gadabout?

In the big picture, it's critical that you don't utilize your flexible time circumstances to procure a couch potato license. Over the long haul, you might want to catch a few reruns of *The Beverly Hillbillies* in the afternoon, or listen to the dulcet tones of Bill Kurtis describing in gruesome detail the most brutal crimes imaginable on *American Justice*, but don't make these entertaining asides part of any daylong marathons. You've got to be active—both physically and mentally—to apply your ample free time to the best of your advantage.

Unemployment Benefit #8

You can finally uncover what all the fuss is about surrounding *Teletubbies* and *Barney & Friends*.

Jobless Action Figure

Plan your work and work your plan. Make this your unemployment mantra. But marry an active job search with corresponding doses of relaxing moments and enlightening endeavors. The truth is that only when you are vigorously and intelligently pursuing your next job can you fully appreciate the benefits of not having a job. Strange as that might sound, it makes sense. In other words, if you feel that you're leaving no stone unturned in bridging the gap between jobs or careers, you'll relish taking a hot shower at one o'clock in the afternoon or feeding the ducks at the zoo in the early morning hours.

EXERCISE
A Jobless Routine Primer

Many unemployment gurus suggest committing four to six hours of your day to the job search. In the end, the allotment of time that you decide to budget to the search will vary from day to day. Nevertheless, a good rule of thumb is to dedicate several quality hours or more to doing what you have to do. What follows is an adaptable script—a jobless routine primer—for you to modify to your unique jobless circumstances:

1. Start your day as early as possible. The human brain tends to be more focused and alert earlier in the day and more tired and distracted later on. Simply put: Always take full advantage of the finite hours of daylight.

2. Develop a job mission statement, summarizing in a sentence or two precisely what you expect to see at the end of

your unemployment rainbow. Review it every morning to reorient yourself to your job search.

3. In the very best cover letters and résumés ever written, document your exceptional human resources. Get them into as many potential job leads' hands as is humanly possible.

4. Apply for jobs via the Internet, which is now chock full of websites that permit you to post your résumé, as well as comprehensive job search engines. Several sites for the unemployed soul's sore eyes include Indeed.com, JobSearch.org, SimplyHired.com, and SnagAJob.com. The latter lists available part-time positions. A program of the United States Department of Commerce that gives you the scoop on open government jobs can be accessed at FedWorld.gov. Also, don't bypass individual company websites, which regularly post open positions at the source. With all the job leads you'll be able to find online, you should have no trouble applying for at least one job each day—make that your goal.

5. Comb the local dailies. Even in the Information Age, job classified ads in black-and-white print are plentiful.

6. Venture out into the open air as early in the day as possible. Apply for jobs in person where possible.

7. Complement your job search, if feasible, with a further education. That is, consider enrolling in night classes at local colleges and universities. Look into job retraining programs offered by state and local governments. Investigate where free courses, workshops, or seminars that are germane to your job search are being held. No matter who you are, and what you do, there are many aspects of your job skills that can be improved upon. In these ever-changing technological

times that we live in, there's always something new for us to learn.

8. Tap into your network on a recurring basis. Keep in close touch with former co-workers, business associates, friends, and family members. The more people out there who know about your present situation, the more chances that a solid lead will come your way. Silence is *not* golden when you're out of a job—quite the contrary.

9. Take plenty of breathers during your job search. Again, it's essential to be active, *but not frenetic*. Keep moving, but keep healthy. Now is not the time to burn out. After you've completed your daily job search duties, relax and relax some more!

10. Exercise whenever and wherever you can.

11. Go to places you wouldn't—or absolutely couldn't—have gone to while dutifully employed.

12. Whatever it takes, avoid becoming a jobless hermit. Make your unemployed routine as people-oriented as possible. Socialize with your immediate family, friends, and former business associates as much as time and good judgment allow.

13. Utilize your evening to review your daily accomplishments. Keep a jobless diary each and every day, chronicling the jobs you've applied for and interviews that you've scheduled and completed, as well as places you've searched for work prospects. Also maintain a section of your jobless diary for an account of the many things you did that were not job-related. Highlight the discoveries that came your way courtesy of being a jobless statistic.

14. Get a good night's rest—you deserve it!

Tips for successfully and happily completing the above activities will be explained in greater detail on the pages to come.

The Résumé: Spend a Lot of Time with It

The most important tool in your job search toolbox is, of course, the résumé. Since sizeable slices of your job search revolve around sending résumés to prospective employers, or looking for good leads on where to send them, it's in your best interests to craft an effective résumé—a potent sales pitch that makes a winning case that you're the right person for the position you are seeking.

Since this chapter's subject matter is grounded in time management and sensible scheduling as they specifically relate to unemployed living, we'd be remiss if we did not spend some time on the résumé. A key component in jobless time management involves putting together a top-notch résumé, yes, but also appreciating the fact that one-size-fits-all is not the best way to go. In other words, it's critical that you tailor your résumé for each and every job of interest to you. This sliver of advice is particularly relevant when you are broadening your horizons and exploring diverse career options.

Emphasize specific skills and accomplishments in your work history that most correspond with the particular position you are after. For example, if you're trying to land a job as editor in a publishing house, highlight your background and achievements as they correlate with the potential job at hand. Do you have a college degree in journalism, creative writing, English, or a related field? The right educational background would obviously help you here. Are you proficient in the ins and outs of grammar, editing, and applicable software programs? This is precisely the kind of know-how that will work in your favor for an editing position. On the other hand, if you are applying for a managerial slot in a financial services company, you'll want to highlight aspects of your education and work credentials that commend you for this role. What have you done that accentuates your capacity to lead people? What special knowledge qualifies you to work in financial services? Make your résumé simultaneously about you and the job you covet.

If, on the other hand, you're venturing into virgin career territory, now is the time to evaluate all that you've heretofore accomplished in past jobs. What skills have you exhibited? What work decisions have you made? How can the weighty sum total of all that you've previously been aid and abet you on your new career path? The answers to these questions should find themselves in your résumé.

The bottom line is that you want to target your résumé to both the particular positions and the particular companies with which you are seeking future employment. This individualizing of your résumé means that you will have to apportion real chunks of time in your daily schedule to tweaking it on a recurrent basis. Foremost, you've got to prepare a foundation résumé, as it were, teeming with your many qualifications: educational training, work history, acquired skills, accomplishments, and goals. Résumé updating should thereafter be a regular part of your routine. And if it gobbles up some serious time, consider it time well spent.

EXERCISE
Résumé Formats

There are various ways to approach the preparation of your résumé. The method you select should be based on who you are, what you've done, and what you want. Here are three widely utilized résumé formats. Choose the one that best suits you.

_____ Chronological

As you've probably guessed, this résumé is based on a chronology of the jobs you've had. By listing your most recently held positions first and then working backwards in time, you give a prospective future employer a clear schematic of the progression of your career. Be sure to:

✦ Include the names and locations of your former employers and dates of employment, along with concise descriptions of your job roles.

✦ Follow your work history with a description of your educational background.

This style of résumé is the most popular. If you've had a consistent work history with no unexplained gaps or wild twists and turns, this is a painless way to go, particularly if your job life reveals real growth on your part—that is, if your progression in jobs demonstrates that you have assumed more responsibilities and realized more accomplishments with time.

_____ Functional

This is a résumé style that underscores your abilities above all else. Functional résumés often begin with an _objective_.

That means that you:

+ First tell a prospective employer what you can offer them.
+ Follow this concise statement with a list of specific job functions.
+ Couple this list with elaborate descriptions of the very things you can do within each job function that make you a valuable human resource.

Examples of job functions include management, editorial, field supervision, communication, and marketing. Highlighting functions in a résumé offers you great versatility, because you can—depending on the job you are applying for—focus on functions that are specific to a prospective employer and the available position. Here again, you've got to tailor your functional résumé for the specific job you are after. This type of résumé also asks that you list past jobs, but doesn't demand the detail of a chronological résumé, because the emphasis here is placed on your skills. It works especially well when you are blazing a new career path and want to emphasize your expertise, not your unrelated past employment. Nevertheless, listing your past jobs is essential. It validates that you've honed your skills in the real world and in some real places.

_____ Combination

The third type of résumé merely combines key aspects of the chronological résumé with the functional résumé. This combination résumé works best when you want to describe your employment experiences (along with names, locations, and dates), but also highlight your special abilities and capacity to excel in certain functions. For instance, there may be one particular job you held that is especially meaningful in light of the one that you're presently seeking. A combination résumé would enable you to chronologically list your previous work history, but also dwell on the particular skills you gathered from one or more of your past jobs.

The Cover Letter: Icing on the Résumé Cake

Your cover letter and résumé are a dynamic duo—Siamese twins. Just as with the résumé, each and every cover letter that you fire off into the wider world should be customized with the recipient in mind. Follow this formula:

+ Devise a couple of paragraphs that sell your qualifications.

+ Individualize this general pitch for the particular company and the specific position you are applying for—always.

+ Repeat this modification process over and over in your job search.

+ Keep in mind that one-size-fits-all cover letters and résumés more often than not end up in the office paper shredder *without being read*, or are dispatched with alacrity into virtual oblivion with a click of a mouse. You are not saving time by sending out mass résumés to multiple prospects—just the opposite. So invest time and research the particulars of the job you are seeking.

+ Investigate what the company offering the job is all about.

+ Look into the industry at large in which this employer conducts business.

In other words, infuse your cover letter with great awareness of the business reality you're trying to break into. Complement this grand knowledge with a concise depiction of your work attributes and why you think you are the best-qualified person for the open job. Let your résumé do the rest of the talking. What you want is the cover letter–résumé one-two punch to land you an interview and put you ever closer to the door prize—a new job.

To further enhance your job search, you should surf the virtual seas and crash into EmploymentSpot.com. Here you'll encounter a comprehensive website loaded with information and tools, including an employment search by city, state, and industry. You'll also chance upon a wealth of very useful articles on matters of importance to the job seeker, including the significance of writing an unbeatable cover letter and résumé.

As a jobless member in good standing, view your cover letter as more important than your résumé in this regard: It's the very first thing a human resources manager will read. In other words, if nobody sees your résumé, its stellar quality means nothing. Your cover letter sets the table. And since you're out of work, take the requisite time—you have plenty of it—to make your cover letter shine. In addition, emphasize the fact that you're between jobs right now and raring to go. This professional hunger and ready availability works in your favor.

Job Interview Prep

Make it part of your daily schedule to keep your job interview skills sharp as a wolf's tooth. That is, along with your daily hunt for work—locating prospects and getting résumés into their hands—plow through possible job interview questions and practice your answers to them. As you go on interviews, keep a record of the questions that were asked of you, paying special attention to the ones that surprised you or caught you off guard. Add them to your job interview tool arsenal for the next go around.

EXERCISE
Job Interview Questions

The corporate bigwigs relish nothing more than making job applicants squirm before them under a fusillade of questions. They enjoy the cat-and-mouse games of trying to trip up interviewees. If you are fully prepared for the job interview fray, however, you'll emerge unscathed and land on two feet. What follows are variations of some typical—and some not so typical—job interview questions:

1. Why are you interested in this particular job?
2. What makes you think you're the most qualified person to fill this open position?
3. What past work experiences have you had that lend themselves to the job you are presently seeking?
4. What level of responsibilities and challenges would satisfy you in your new job?
5. Describe what you deem your biggest accomplishments in past jobs? Your biggest failures?
6. What do you see as your most preeminent skills?
7. What areas of your skills would you like to improve upon?
8. Describe the toughest decisions you've had to make while in past jobs, and what were the results of these decisions?
9. How do you feel you react in pressure-packed situations? Can you cite any examples from your work past to back this up?

10. Do you consider yourself a team player? What situations from your previous work experiences showcase your capacity to get along with others in a productive way?

11. Do you have leadership qualities? When, in past jobs, did you exhibit the capacity to lead others?

12. Is there a manager or supervisor from your past whom you respect above all others? If so, what were the qualities that you most admired?

13. Do you consider monetary compensation more important in your career than job challenges and responsibilities?

14. Are there certain responsibilities and challenges that you'd like in the job you are interviewing for that you never experienced in past positions?

15. What are your short-term and long-term career-oriented goals?

Invest some quality time in interview nuts and bolts

As we wrap up this important topic, there are some job interview nuts and bolts that are worth mentioning here. You may think some of these points are incredibly obvious, or even trivial, but they are imperative nonetheless. A small act—a subtle thing you *do* or *don't do* in an interview—could swing the pendulum in your favor, or implode your chances altogether in securing the job you're after. Use your unemployment freedom to fully prepare for interviews. You have no excuse for not being on the top of your game.

Here are several key matters to carefully consider during the job interview process:

✦ **Don't behave like a stick in the mud.** Don't forget to exhibit vital signs during the entire length of the interview. You're supposed to be enthusiastic about the prospective job and working for the interviewer's company.

✦ **Your eyes have it.** Look the interviewer in the eyes. It sounds like a trifling point, but it's not.

✦ **Dress for success.** Look your best. Smell your best. But in the end, don't overdo anything from makeup to cologne to unpleasant-smelling mouthwash (like Listerine). Also, this isn't the best time to express your individuality by sporting a Mohawk hairdo or wearing a nose ring.

✦ **Be confident, sell yourself, but avoid crossing that fine line into braggadocio or bizarreness.** You're hoping to get hired. So, selling yourself like Billy Mays pitches Kaboom! or Mighty Putty is not the way to go here.

✦ **Prepare questions to ask your prospective employer.** During the interview, you are customarily asked if you have any questions about the available job and the company offering it. So, ask about the specifics of the job—what you will have to do on a regular basis. Naturally, interviewers expect prospective employees to want to know these things. They also count on them being capable of having a give-and-take conversation. Ask your prospective employer questions like these: *What are the company's strengths and weaknesses vis-à-vis the competition in the marketplace? Exactly what kind of work will I be doing on a day-to-day basis? How does the company encourage the development and realization of career goals? What kinds of decisions will I be asked to make in my job role? What qualities do you think make for an ideal employee? How and when will my performance be measured?*

EXERCISE
Jobless Schedule Blueprint

If you feel a routine without any precise parameters is counterproductive—that it would cause you to drift—then by all means work with a more prearranged schedule. Set starting times and time frames for your daily life as an unemployed individual. Highlight the key facets of your days, and time you wish to allot them. Living a new kind of life (for the time being anyway) and looking for a new job or career can be daunting. A schedule to follow often helps in maintaining order and keeping your feet to the job search fire.

What follows are some scheduling parameters for you to work with. Feel free to change their order on the list or excise the ones that don't apply, as well as add new items to the mix. Or, if the idea of keeping a schedule during your break from the rat race quite frankly makes your stomach turn, feel free to tear the following section right out of the book. (Okay, maybe not really.) Remember, though, that it pays to establish a positive routine while out of work. You don't want to develop bad habits and fritter the days away. It's so easy to do. Be productive and aware at all times of what you're doing and what you want to accomplish.

Morning Rise Hour: _____

Shower and Dress Time: _____ to _____

Breakfast Preparation and Eating Time: _____ to _____

Morning Internet Job Search Time: _____ to _____

Morning Newspaper and Periodical Job Search Time:
_____ to _____

Résumé/Cover Letter Preparation and Tweaking Time:
_____ to _____

Résumé/Cover Letter E-Mailing and Mailing Time:
_____ to _____

Morning In-Person Job Search Time: _____ to _____

Morning Exercise and Leisure Pursuits Time:
_____ to _____

Lunch Break: _____ to _____

Afternoon Internet Job Search Time (optional):
_____ to _____

Afternoon Exercise and Leisure Pursuits Time:
_____ to _____

Grocery Shopping Time: _____ to _____

Dinner Preparation and Eating Time: _____ to _____

Evening Exercise and Leisure Pursuits Time: _____ to _____

Bedtime Hour: _____

Throughout your jobless stint, utilize your afternoons—a fair portion of them anyway—to have a grand old time and ward off the blues. In fact, subsequent chapters are loaded with possibilities to do just that and keep you clear-headed throughout your job search. Take a gander at chapters five, six, seven, and twelve for some intriguing ideas to plug into your afternoons.

Unemployment Benefit #9

You can eat your breakfast in bed ... and lunch ... and dinner, too.

Ten Ways to Make Certain You Get Out of the House Every Day

The chief reason why a good number of unemployed men and women choose to work with a more-or-less set schedule is that they want to make certain they get out of the house every single day. Sure, they want to look for work, too, but so much of the job search these days can be undertaken at home via the computer and the telephone. Compelling yourself to leave the house on a regular basis is a positive thing on numerous levels.

Fending off depression and a sense of hopelessness is reason enough to trek out into open air as much as is realistically possible. Do as many things away from the home fires as you can logically fit into the day. Commingle with the masses. Meet with family, friends, or former co-workers for lunch. Go to the library for job research purposes or leisure reading. Just keep active and in perpetual motion.

What follows are ten possibilities for you to weigh that'll ensure you get out of the house on a day-to-day basis.

1. Walk or Jog for Exercise and Relaxation.

Start it all from your front door, or take it to a unique location like a park or track at a nearby school. Try to appreciate distinct things about your environment each time you venture out.

2. Visit a Gym for a Regular Workout.

Stretching your body stretches your mind too. Talk to one new person each time you go (but not in a crazy, I'm-desperate-for-human-contact kind of way. Play it cool, okay?).

3. Meet a Member of Your Life Network.

That is, get together for a cup of coffee or lunch with a relative, friend, or former business associate. Put a high premium on seeing and speaking with genuine flesh-and-blood folks every single day. Stay connected with people on a social level, as well as maintain regular contact with individuals who may furnish you with a job lead that turns out to be *the* job lead.

4. Volunteer Your Time with a Charitable Organization or Another Institution.

There are a lot of people in the world and an unfortunate number of them are in need of a pair of helping hands. Strange as this may ring to the ears, volunteering (for absolutely no compensation) is often a rewarding experience for an unemployed soul (in need of paying work).

5. Take a Part-time Job.

Even if your immediate financial straits could tide you over for a while, it's sometimes beneficial to assume a temporary job for several hours every day, just to remain active and focused. And the part-time paycheck can only help!

6. Depending on Your Educational Background, Consider Tutoring Kids.

It's no stretch to say that today's youth are knowledge-deficient in many areas (for example, they think Abraham Lincoln communicated via cell phone with General Grant!). On top of everything else, private tutors charge $50 to $100 an hour.

7. Babysit Friends' Kids.

Or, provide home care to a senior citizen in need of assistance (such as grocery shopping, cleaning, or meal preparation). Word of mouth in your neighborhood or via the channels of your social network can often find you informal jobs in this busy bailiwick.

8. Visit the Library or, Better Yet, Libraries.

These are ideal locations for unearthing job research tools, but also prime places to read up on just about anything imaginable. Free access to books, magazines, periodicals, and more is nothing to sniff at!

9. Shop for Your Next Meals.

Grocery shopping on a daily basis gets you out of the house and, among other places, into supermarkets full of foods and people. Just for fun, pretend to stock the shelves and count how many people—confusing you for an employee (oh, the irony)—approach you with questions about the store. (If nothing else, this will be good practice for when you really *do* have a job.)

10. Visit Local Landmarks.

No, this doesn't mean you need to hike to the top of the Empire State Building or call on George Washington's birthplace. Just go to places in your neck of the woods every single day that you've never before patronized. Maybe there are obscure parks nearby that you've not experienced, or an old diner you've passed a thousand times on the way to work. When we're employed, we regularly bypass living and breathing landmarks. And we're not talking about locales on the National Register of Historic Places here. We're interested in locations and establishments that are nearby with a welcome mat out for you. You've got no excuses now.

Your Next Job: So What's It Going to Be?

The past is not your potential.

In any hour you can choose to liberate the future.

—Marilyn Ferguson

Voluntarily leaving your job, or involuntarily losing one, puts you in the unenviable position of not having a regular source of income. You can take this statement to the bank without, alas, your weekly paycheck. But the loss of a job simultaneously places you in the *enviable* circumstances of being the master of your destiny. Sometimes it's merely a matter of you seeing your glass as half full rather than half empty.

Granted, for many living and breathing statistics in the jobless community—and you may very well be among this honored brood—a stretch of unemployment is not exactly cause for dancing in the streets or popping of champagne corks. Being the engineer of your life train doesn't automatically mean you are as happy as a feline in a field full of catnip. No, charting your future course can be extraordinarily stressful at times. It is often fraught with bumps, potholes, and seemingly intractable obstacles. But now is certainly not the time to veer off course into the jobless traveler's equivalent of the Bermuda Triangle. Rather, take full stock of where you are right now and decide what direction you want to go in ... *and go.* It is often that simple.

The Unemployment Inventory

As a young man, American business legend Walt Disney lost a job at an advertising agency. In fact, the man behind the prolific, internationally renowned animations of Mickey Mouse, Donald Duck, et al, was deemed utterly lacking in artistic acumen. Disney recounted the story of his getting the old heave-ho at this place of employment. He not only got fired, he remembered, but the higher-ups in the agency told him point-blank that he exhibited "a singular lack of drawing ability."

Perhaps you can readily identify with Walt Disney's past predicament. That is, you're feeling kind of down about your chosen career field and don't know if you want to continue in it. Maybe you're thinking that it's not the perfect match for your particular abilities and unique passions. Then again, you might have been toiling in recent jobs that were just not your cup of tea and, beyond a scintilla of doubt, you recognize that a change of life plan is in order. Well, this is the ideal moment to either right a wrong course or chart an entirely new one.

It's high time to take stock of your personal inventory from head to toe. Reach deep down into your innards and assess your special job skills, exceptional talents, distinguishing interests, particular life passions, and, of course, your educational background.

EXERCISE
Unemployment Inventory Quiz

In order to facilitate an appropriate personal inventory during this jobless period in your life, there is a battery of questions that you should ask yourself. But more importantly, you've got to honestly answer them. The final step involves rolling them over into a rewarding job, career path, or new business. Here they are:

1. What do you feel are your most priceless job-specific skills? In other words, what can you offer a prospective employer that makes you stand out from the pack?

   _____

   _____

2. What special talents do you possess beyond job-specific skills that possibly can be applied to forging a new career or entrepreneurial endeavor?

   _____

   _____

3. What unique interests define your everyday life? More specifically:

   Where do you go for fun? _____

   What kinds of books do you read?_____

   What kinds of magazines do you subscribe to? ____

   What do you watch on television? _____

   What movies do you watch? _____

   What do you eat? Where do you eat? _____

   What are your hobbies? _____

   What catches your eye? _____

4. What are the things you're most passionate about in life? Can you translate any of these particular passions into a satisfying job, career, or business?

    _____

    _____

5. Are your educational background and work history validations of your talents and interests? (If they aren't, might you consider going back to school or changing career paths and possibly finding a completely different line of work?)

    _____

    _____

Now take this personal inventory to the next level with these more direct questions about a job, career, or business:

1. Are you interested in being your own boss?

    _____

2. Do you consider yourself a "people person" who works well with others? (This could include everything from managing a department for somebody else to running your very own customer-oriented business.)

    _____

3. Are you looking for work possibilities with a wide upside for advancement?

    _____

4. Do you have a particular income figure in mind for your next job?

    _____

Do you have another one for five years in the future?

_____

And five years after that?

_____

5. Are you concerned about job security above all else? (That is, do you want to avoid working in a company—or industry— where your job could be downsized or outsourced at the drop of a hat?)

_____

6. Do you have at the top of your work agenda real responsibilities and genuine challenges? (Or do you prefer to go with the flow?)

_____

7. Are you looking for work that interests you beyond a juicy paycheck? In other words, do you want to be involved in a job, career, or business that excites you on a personal level?

_____

8. On which of the following do you put a higher premium?
   _____A. Leisure time and spending quality time with your family.
   _____B. Plugging away at your work-related responsibilities.

9. Do you want to forge a career that gives something back to your community or society at large? In other words, would you like to help people for a living?

_____

10. Are you interested in blazing a trail or leaving a stamp of some kind behind in your work life?

_____

You've now completed your unemployment inventory. What do your answers to the questions above tell you about your employment preferences? Looking back on your last job, did it mesh well with all of your preferences? If not, what can you do to make sure you get it right the next time around?

Grab hold of this mother lode of insight into the core of your being—it'll come in quite handy on your job safari.

The Career Love Connection

Granted, it's painting with a rather broad brush, but it's probably fair to conclude that society at large doesn't truly encourage imagination and the realization of one's full potential. Our special aptitudes and human possibilities are not routinely nurtured. Sure, there's a lot of lip service given to realizing one's dreams and all of that, but when you cut to the chase, it's mostly empty rhetoric.

And yes, it's often our well-meaning—and sometimes not so well-meaning—families who command the dream-squashing brigades. Hey, the bottom line is so often *the bottom line*. Most of us are raised in environments with encouragement to—foremost—bring home the bacon. And this discussion isn't meant to affix blame on the state of modern-day parenting, despite the reality that many parents put an explicit emphasis on making the green before living the dream. We can't live, after all, without money and a steady stream of it.

Unfortunately, there's a noxious flip side to this placement of money-making atop the societal pedestal. In all too many instances, this money-amounts-to-success belief system casts people adrift. In other words, many of us never get a chance to fulfill our true potentials, or experience authentic satisfaction, because life has this uncanny knack of tying us up with commitments and responsibilities that often preclude seismic career moves and such. But the truth is we can have both a rewarding career *and* the dollars to meet our personal commitments and relish the many things that only money can buy. They are not—by a long shot—mutually exclusive.

The Unemployment Benefit of Free Love

Since you're unemployed—and free to be bold—take this opportunity to unearth work that truly satisfies you—and, yes, pays you a living wage or, better yet, makes you a mint. And let's make this crystal clear right now: The money you make, or have in the bank—or don't make or don't have in the bank—is not the barometer of your character. Nevertheless, it's not a character assassin, either. In fact, all things being equal, we'd all just as soon land a rewarding job or career path that simultaneously brings in some big bucks.

While mulling over your next career move, it helps to look into the jobs and industries that are considered promising in the current climate. The more real-life career ideas that you encounter, the better feel you'll have for what's in front of you and where you want to go from here. So, take your wide-ranging unemployment inventory and match it up against *U.S. News and World Report*'s list of the best careers in 2007:

+ Audiologist
+ Biomedical equipment technician
+ Clergy
+ Curriculum/training specialist
+ Dentist
+ Editor

+ Engineer
+ Firefighter
+ Fundraiser
+ Genetic counselor
+ Ghostwriter
+ Government manager
+ Hairstylist/cosmetologist
+ Higher education administrator
+ Investment banker
+ Landscape architect
+ Librarian
+ Locksmith/security system technician
+ Management consultant
+ Mediator
+ Occupational therapist
+ Optometrist
+ Pharmacist
+ Physician assistant
+ Politician/elected official
+ Professor
+ Registered nurse
+ School psychologist
+ Systems analyst
+ Urban planner
+ Usability/user experience specialist

For more in-depth details on the specific careers that made the cut—what they are and why they were selected—call upon USNews.com and commence a search for "best careers." The news magazine's website also has some highly informative and interesting articles on specific jobs and career paths, as well as materials on undertaking the more general career search. In addition, there are several websites that enable you to match your personal inventory of skills, passions, and life commitments with careers. In other words, you plug in all the information about what makes you tick, and in return you get a list of careers that are the perfect fit. For starters, try LiveCareer.com, ProjectCareer.com, and CareerTest. us. Keep in mind that career-matching tests are not scientific. They are meant to—above all else—supply you with some food for thought. You might be surprised at some of the career suggestions that come your way based on your individual profile. A couple of other virtual locales worth visiting for career fodder and actual job possibilities are Job.com and Beyond.com. The latter bills itself as "the largest niche career network" in cyberspace. You be the judge.

Off the Beaten Trail: A New Approach to the Job Hunt

Work life has long been branded as "the rat race." But no one can deny that the present-day rat race has taken on a whole new rodent-like dimension. In fact, you could say that the contemporary rat race is spreading the workplace equivalent of the bubonic plague. With outsourcing and downsizing becoming very real concerns for more and more Americans, the labor market is in a perpetual state of flux. Nowadays, most large corporations compete globally. To facilitate these international pursuits, they must be mean and lean, which is bad news for a lot of people who rely on a living wage for basic sustenance.

This job marketplace reality reveals—among many things—that the most popular careers of today are not the most popular careers of fifty years ago, ten years ago, or even a couple years ago. With the technological train leaving the station on a recurrent basis, you most certainly have to be on your toes to compete in the existing rat race and have any reasonable chance of crossing the finish line. But, hey, you aren't a rat, so why re-enter the rat race as just described? You have alternatives. And now is as good a time as any to exercise your options. Move forward into a job, career, or business that shields you from the proverbial rat droppings we've just depicted.

By employing a non-traditional approach to searching for your next line of work, you will increase your chances of achieving what you genuinely want and genuinely deserve in a paying job, long-term career, or business of your own. Foremost, it's critical that you appreciate the fundamental realities of the present, such as:

+ **A college degree isn't always what it's cracked up to be.** Ironically, with a college education pushed as the surest route to so-called success, a shortage has arisen in many blue-collar careers where hands-on skills are required. And, simultaneously, many college graduates—with sheepskins hanging proudly on their walls—are finding that their job prospects are rather slim pickings. So, if you've got unmistakable aptitudes, such as the capacity to fix things—e.g., plumbing, electrical, carpentry, or mechanical—why not appraise the many career possibilities that exist here? Have you noticed what plumbers charge per hour these days? And how they are so often hard to reach? The last time you visited an auto mechanic, what did it cost you to have your vehicle tuned up? Skilled tradespeople are in big demand.

+ **Off-shoring of work is catching a lot of people in its riptide.** So, why pursue a career in an area subject to the mercurial whims of bloodless corporations only interested in the bottom line, not the well-being of you and yours? Ponder this: If the work you've previously toiled in involved computer and telephone duties—and nothing else—it fits the job outsourcing profile to a tee.

✦ **Being green is bringing in the green.** Environmentally friendly products and services are unquestionably getting more and more traction in the general economy. Going green is definitely the wave of the future and not some momentary fad. Green careers and green businesses are not about to turn brown with the passage of time—quite the contrary.

✦ **Senior power is getting more senior with each passing day.** We are living in an increasingly older society. The baby boom generation is graying and slowly but surely shuffling off into their well-earned retirements. Couple this demographic fact of life with significant advancements in medical technology and medicines and the end result is that people are living longer and longer. This means that there is a rising demand for senior products and services, including in-home *non-medical* care.

✦ **Another day, another weak dollar.** The U.S. dollar is not as mighty as it once was. This amounts to foreign currencies being able to afford and thus purchase more American products than ever before. Businesses and careers with an exporting component (or the sole component) are something to seriously contemplate. Let the world be your oyster, as it were.

✦ **The consequence of knowledge has just gotten more consequential.** If you have knowledge to pass on, or to spare, you might want to sample the teaching profession. We need to know even more these days to compete in the fast-paced, highly technical world marketplace. Yet, good teachers are on the endangered species list. In addition, with increasing numbers of jobs being done by machines these days, there is a growing need for technicians to lord over these automatons. If you have proficiency in these quarters, you are a precious human resource indeed.

✦ **Supply doesn't equal demand when it comes to sales representatives.** According to U.S. Department of Labor, the position of sales representative accounts for the top talent shortage in the entire country.

✦ **Government jobs offer more security than most others.** If financial security is highest on your agenda, you could do worse than working for a government institution, be it on the local, state, or federal level. There are *always* available jobs on all levels in all areas of government.

✦ **Crafting a business and career has just gotten more promising.** The arts and crafts market is blossoming beyond recognition. It is unfurling its welcome mat and embracing entrepreneurs with wide-ranging talents in making things ranging from jewelry to handbags to hand-blown glass. Check out the business of crafting in action at Etsy.com, which bills itself as "Your place to buy and sell all things handmade."

✦ **Some trades are recession-proof—or pretty close to it.** The pet care industry, for example, is not only on the rise, but also impervious to the slings and arrows of the temperamental business cycle. In fact, there are slices of this commercial trade that are embracing disaffected members of the rat race. That is, many men and women are exiting jobs in the dog-eat-dog corporate world to initiate things like doggie daycares and pet-sitting businesses.

To further augment your education of the current career and labor market landscapes, here are several websites replete with up-to-the-minute information on all that's transpiring in the world of people earning their livings and, in fact, looking for ways to earn their livings: Vault.com, MarketWatch.com, FastCompany.com, JobHunt.org, and Entrepreneur.com. You'll encounter a treasure trove of articles on copious topics in the area of careers, available jobs, business trends, and what's hot and what's not—you name it. And while on this important topic, you'd be remiss if you didn't check out the U.S. Department of Labor's *Occupational Outlook Handbook* at bls.gov/oco. Regularly updated, this is considered the Bible of career information. When all is said and done, just keep in mind what Confucius once said: "Choose a job you love and you will never have to work a day in your life."

Five Ways to Make Sure the Job Search Doesn't Take Over Your Life

A supreme life irony is that the workday—which fast becomes the work week and then the work year—quite often comes attached to a pair of blinders. The day-to-day work slog frequently compresses the wider world into a narrow tunnel—a one-way street that invariably leads to a dead end or, worse still, a boulevard of broken dreams. This stark reality is precisely why jobless stints are frequently eye-openers and, in some instances, liberators.

Whether or not your recent work experiences fit into the description just laid out, you are, nevertheless, temporarily out of the job loop. So, whether it's traipsing off to the salt mine to earn a buck every day, or searching for work on the highways and byways—which is your job right now—it's imperative that you not get consumed by the process.

What follows are several possibilities for you to consider that can assist you in getting through the job pursuit in one piece—physically as well as emotionally.

1. **Take off the work blinders while you're unemployed.** Courtesy of your surplus hours of jobless free time, you are afforded one golden opportunity after another to do things you've never done before and to go places you've never gone before. In other words, complement your job search with a heaping helping of pleasure. Numerous unemployed folks find that they can marry their job quests with ample doses of productive leisure activities. For example, they attend job interviews while simultaneously exploring the physical surroundings of where those interviews come to pass. That is, a job interview may transpire in a high-rise building, but ordinarily that imposing edifice calls home a unique neighborhood with more to offer than steel girders, Plexiglas windows, elevator rides, and people running around like chickens with their heads cut off.

2. **Look upon your unemployment as a lifestyle segue.** Use your newfound free time—however fleeting it is—to usher in a new and improved lifestyle that you'll never cast aside. Maximize your unemployed days and nights and assume positive habits and attitudes that are both portable and applicable to the next phase of your life—whatever it happens to be—and the one after that as well.

3. **Get in touch with your inner Bob Vila and Martha Stewart.** There is no better time than now to tackle the subject of getting your house in order—literally. For all too many of us, home

repairs and major cleaning efforts are often relegated to those ubiquitous to-do lists. Lists, by the way, which keep growing and growing while the mission-accomplished check boxes remain blank. In keeping with the abiding theme found throughout this entire book, it's a good thing to get into good habits while unemployed. By utilizing a slice of your jobless timetable to fix things up and clean up some messes, you will not only make your home more functional, you'll feel better about yourself, too. Depending on your particular life circumstances, there are multiple tasks you can perform to release the Bob Vila and Martha Stewart within you, including:

✦ Painting a room (or better yet, rooms)
✦ Cleaning out a closet (or better yet, closets)
✦ Dusting places both in view and out of sight
✦ Washing floors
✦ Washing curtains and window blinds
✦ Shampooing a rug
✦ Trimming shrubs and weeding the lawn
✦ Planting a garden
✦ Repairing things that need repairing

Plot your next life act from an orderly and accessible abode, and not a grubby, broken down hovel, even—and this is important—if you reside in a veritable hole in the wall. Physical order goes hand-in-glove with psychological and emotional order. You needn't ever let the unemployment scene get you down and dirty.

4. **A jobless mind is a terrible thing to waste.** While walking on the sedentary side of Unemployment Street, you might want to drop by your local library or neighborhood bookstore. Catch up on your reading, because the beauty of the written word is multifaceted and a potential elixir for what ails you. Think about it: You can at once bolster your search for jobs and careers in the aforementioned establishments, while simultaneously making yourself more erudite and informed on a wide range of topics. Take advantage of the big-box retail bookstores. Not only do these bookshop behemoths have what could best be described as a *title* wave of merchandise, they are also customer-friendly in policy. That is, you can not only patronize these locations to purchase books, but you can lounge around the places, reading to your heart's content in cozy beanbag chairs. It's a library experience with all the comforts of home, sans all of those *please be quiet* recriminations. Use these superstores to investigate new jobs, career paths, and present moneymaking opportunities, and—above all else—have a grand old time.

5. **Visit museums whenever and wherever you can.** Why not budget a handful of your jobless hours to museum visits? Sure, it sounds a bit trite to suggest such a thing. However, the reality is that most of us are missing out on seeing and experiencing a wealth of truly compelling and enlightening places. And, on top of that, museums can offer promising ideas and possibilities for subsequent job prospects and career moves.

Just take all of the job-search detours! Sure, you won't exactly know where you'll come out, but the odds are they'll be worthwhile destinations. And they'll help you both survive *and thrive* the job chase.

PART TWO

HAVING A BLAST

Twenty Fun Activities You Can Do for Free

The best things in life are free.

—American proverb

In the understandably uneasy and wholly unpredictable world of joblessness, it's not surprising that many souls among the unemployed fraternity put having a good time on the back burner. Nevertheless, this is a time in your life when you have more time, as it were, to do things that you couldn't do while you were working. And, of course, to do things that you didn't do while holding a full-time job, because they just never occurred to you. So, look upon the following roster of twenty fun activities, which you can do for free (or next to nothing), as unemployment benefits that'll enhance your future job prospects, if only because of the reduced stress they are almost sure to bring your way.

You might want to consider these activities as just compensation for all of the physical and mental fuel you are dispensing in the demanding job search:

1. Do the Daily Crossword Puzzle in the Newspaper

If you purchase the newspaper every day at a newsstand, or have it delivered to your doorstep each morning, don't bypass the whopping educational and fun activity at your fingertips—the crossword puzzle. Working crosswords on a regular basis stimulates your brain and bolsters your attention span, two attributes that can nobly assist you in your job search. On top of everything else, you learn a lot of new words and phrases by completing crossword puzzles. You can also find free crossword puzzles on various websites, including JustCrosswords.com and BestCrosswords.com.

A couple of footnotes here: If you read your newspapers at the local library, make a copy of the crossword puzzle. It is not good form to deface a library copy of a newspaper—or anything else in that hallowed place! Also, feel free to do the Sudoku puzzles as well.

2. Go on Neighborhood Walking Tours

It's been previously touched upon in the pages of this book that you've been handed a rare opportunity along with your pink slip. Now that you're certifiably—albeit temporarily—unemployed, you can explore places you've never before had the time, or the inclination, to explore. Why not take walking tours of the neighborhoods in your neck of the woods, or, perhaps, the neighborhoods where you are interviewing or looking for a job?

There are unique neighborhoods in all locations of the country. You might be surprised at the things to see, and the things to do, in places that are geographically very close to you, but might as well have been in outer Mongolia while you toiled in a nine-to-five job—or, more likely, a nine-to-six job.

3. Sample Bizarre Foods

Take a prompt from chef Andrew Zimmern's popular program on the Travel Channel, *Bizarre Foods*. Zimmern travels the planet to sample local foods that most of us might deem a wee bit strange, like barbecued cow scrotum and still-beating frog hearts. But Zimmern has also called on American terra firma with some pretty unusual fare.

Since you have to eat lunch anyway, why not broaden your horizons by trying some foods that you never before considered? You don't have to go the fantastic lengths of Zimmern. Maybe ordering a shish kebab from a street vendor is bizarre enough for you. This bizarre food adventure can be blazed in supermarkets and specialty groceries, too, which offer all sorts of free samples. If you've long resisted sampling some of these complimentary mouthfuls—because of their weirdness—now is the time to go for it. In addition, don't turn down any dinner invitations because of the potential bizarre fare that could be served.

Unemployment Benefit #10

Rather than sampling the concoctions that your colleagues bring in for lunch, you can try bizarre foods of your own choosing.

4. Nurture Your Family Tree

Genealogical research is becoming increasingly popular with the hoi polloi. So, while you're job-hunting, you might want to allocate some time for piecing together your family history. Get in touch with relatives for missing pieces of the puzzle. Visit websites like FamilySearch.org to further aid and abet your mission.

This return to your roots can pay you rich dividends down the road, as you can pass on your genealogical finds to the next generation. While treading the path of your genealogical studies, you can simultaneously increase the size of your network. In other words, you'll be in close contact with more and more people. One of these persons may hold the key that unlocks the door to your next job or career.

5. Go Hiking

No matter where you call home—a thriving metropolis, a bedroom community in suburbia, or a sleepy small town—there are more than likely locations nearby with circuitous trails through woodlands or indigenous shrubbery. A rather comprehensive website can be accessed at Local-Hikes.com. Here you'll unearth a wealth of trails not too far from where the post office delivers your mail.

6. Take Free Courses

Comb the newspapers, peruse library and bookstore bulletin boards, and look elsewhere for advertisements for free courses, workshops, lectures, and seminars. If you've never before had your eye out for these kinds of things, you'll be pleasantly surprised at what's going on at nearby colleges and universities, bookstores, and learning annexes.

The topics of these free activities vary considerably. (There are also many courses and seminars that charge fees for the privilege of attending.) Some of the courses might directly assist you in locating your next job, or help you chart an entirely new career path.

7. Read a Good Book

This recommendation is an old favorite. Often during our work slog, time, energy, and desire do not allow for a good read. So, with your excuse book running on empty at the moment, now is the time to take a genuine book out of the library—or grab one from your bookshelf that's been sitting unread and gathering dust—and start reading. Read a book in lieu of excessive television viewing and aimless surfing on the Internet. Not only is reading typically enlightening in some way, but the undertaking itself increases your concentration abilities. This feat is a windfall for your overall psyche, which will benefit you immeasurably in your job search.

Unemployment Benefit #11

Instead of observing pigeons on the ledge of a twentieth floor window in an overcrowded office building in a grimy metropolis, you can go bird-watching in the bosom of Mother Nature.

8. Go Bird-Watching

Take to the local parklands and check out the many winged creatures singing in the trees, soaring through the air, and gliding across bodies of water. You'd be amazed how many people become bird-watching aficionados once they get a taste of it. At Birding.com, you'll encounter much of what you need to know on the subject of bird-watching, aka birding, including bird-watching hotspots and checklists of birds in your own backyard.

9. Write a Novel

Put pen to paper and write that epic novel. You know, the one you've long been writing in your head. Or, maybe, you've got the next *Harry Potter* series of books in mind. You don't even have to shoot for the stars here. In fact, you'd probably be satisfied with penning the next *Lemony Snicket: A Series of Unfortunate Events*.

In any event, if you both commence and complete a full-length novel, there are literary agents who just might be interested in what you've hatched from your exceedingly creative jobless mindset.

10. Keep a Journal

If writing a novel isn't for you, why not keep a daily journal? Spend some time each and every day documenting everything from the weather to your job-hunting hits and misses to your innermost feelings about all that's transpiring during your unemployment odyssey.

Journal writing serves as psychological catharsis. It also improves your communication skills, which—by the way—are highly coveted in the workplace. And, last but not least, a journal leaves a written record of your life and times for posterity.

11. Become a Shutterbug

If you've got a camera—preferably a digital one (no photo developing costs)—take it with you on both your job safari and leisure adventures. Take pictures of people, places, and things. Get a shot of the sunset. Take shots of neighborhood hotspots. Snap photos of family and friends. Record your unemployment days and nights in pictures. It's a wonderful extracurricular activity that could very possibly transcend your joblessness.

If you want to add more clarity to this developing image, so to speak, visit the New York Institute of Photography at NYIP.com, which offers online courses in this picture-perfect discipline. You can augment your current skills as an amateur photographer, or go the distance and become a professional. For a hodgepodge of photography contests—for amateurs and professionals alike—check out ProofPositive.com and PhotoAwards.com.

Unemployment Benefit #12

You can take your camcorder out and about in the great outdoors, patiently wait for someone to fall down and embarrass himself or herself, and promptly pack the video off to *America's Funniest Home Videos.*

12. Volunteer Your Time

Volunteer at a local hospital, nursing home, school, or some other institution looking for help. Participate in a book-reading or after-school program. Join a volunteer fire brigade. You can't ever go wrong by giving something back to the community. In addition, volunteering your time—from time to time—whilst you are unemployed increases your visibility and your network. You now have more people invested in the ultimate success of your job search.

So, if you've been sitting on the volunteer fence, now is the time to remove the splinters from you know where and volunteer somewhere—wherever strikes your fancy. You might consider becoming a Big Brother or Big Sister. Visit BBBSA.org to learn more. In this volunteer sphere, a more general worthwhile website to check out is DoSomething.org. Here you'll encounter a search button that enables you to locate, via your zip code, volunteer opportunities close to home. This outfit is nonpartisan with no agenda. It's all about volunteering somewhere—period.

13. Go Dumpster Diving

Okay, so maybe you shouldn't physically climb into any garbage dumpsters, although some people do. (Number one: It could be dangerous. Number two: It's actually against the law in many places to be crawling around in other people's refuse.) Nevertheless, dumpster diving—and just plain old garbage picking—has a long and vaunted tradition.

The bottom line is that people toss out things of real value. Many items found in the garbage end up on the eBay auction block. But other than stuff to peddle on eBay, there are lots of things thrown away that you could use. Many people find furniture that they refinish. Working lamps are regularly put out by the curbside. Ditto perfectly good rugs. Traverse your neighborhood on garbage pick-up dates and look for bits and pieces that you could take home and use, or, perhaps, sell on eBay or in a yard sale. Garbage picking is both a fun and potentially profitable activity. Just be sure to wash your hands thoroughly after any of these adventures.

14. Write Letters to Famous People

Okay, so you'll have to expend a few stamps to execute this fun activity. That said, writing letters to famous people has a long and storied tradition. So, during your jobless stint, why don't you just sit right down and write yourself a letter . . . to somebody prominent.

You could write a letter to your representative in Congress, or to a U.S. senator, about a burning issue that concerns you—perhaps on the subject of unemployment and the extension of jobless benefits. Send the correspondence to your congressional representative addressed to the Honorable John Doe, c/o United States House of Representatives, Washington, D.C. 20515; or to your senator addressed to the Honorable Jane Doe, c/o United States Senate, Washington, D.C. 20510. For more specific information on who's who in the Congress—perhaps you don't know who your representatives are—visit House.gov and Senate.gov.

You could also pen a fan letter to a favorite actor, musician, or athlete. In fact, why not write a bunch of letters to a bunch of famous folks? Request their autographs while you're at it—very politely, of course. Granted, some of your letter-writing requests will go unanswered; others might come back with autopen autographs (looking authentic, but the work of machines). However, on occasion, you'll get bona fide personal responses and genuine autographs too. For Hollywood celebrity addresses, try Seeing-Stars.com, which maintains a rather large database. Another website with free access to a pantheon of celebrity addresses—from actors to athletes to authors—is CelebritiesFans.com.

Receiving responses to your letter-writing campaign is always exciting. It's a great activity to do with youngsters. But, really, letter writing knows no age restrictions. Going to your mailbox and eyeing a piece of mail that's not a bill or junk mail is welcome correspondence indeed.

Unemployment Benefit #13

In stark contrast to your national government, you can learn to live within a tight budget.

15. Make a Video for YouTube

If you've got a camcorder, you could rather effortlessly make a video and post it on YouTube.com for the entire world to see. Depending on your personality, you might want to produce a spoof on your current state of joblessness, or, perhaps, play it straight and pitch yourself to the viewing audience as a prime piece of job timber.

Of course, you could also place a video on YouTube that chronicles one of your bird-watching adventures or nature-trail expeditions. There are very few boundaries in this visual milieu in cyberspace—even good taste isn't required. This brand of activity on your part could also increase the size of that network we keep mentioning. You might, too, be awakening the Steven Spielberg within you—who knows?

16. Play Some Card Games

This may not sound as daring and as interesting as producing a feature film to post on YouTube, or even walking through the woodlands and spotting a snapping turtle in complete repose on a nearby stone, but card playing is nothing to sniff at as a free and fun activity.

In fact, cards and card games have taken on a whole new dimension in recent times, with more and more persons of all ages getting in on the pastime. For a cornucopia of card-game rules, the history of various card games, and, indeed, access to many free online card games, visit The House of Cards at TheHouseOfCards.com. And, as an intriguing alternative to playing cards for money, you might consider playing *coupon poker*. Peel a page out of *Mr. Mom's* book and go for broke. Use coupons in lieu of cash. It's the perfect card game for an unemployed soul like yourself. That is, playing with coupons keeps the game interesting—with certifiable stakes—while not impacting your bottom line, which is probably more aptly described these days as a bottom-bottom line.

17. Hit the Road Running

Jogging is an activity that you can really get into—and it's good for your overall health and wellness, too. That is, of course, if you don't opt to run alongside traffic jams or during ozone alert days in the summertime.

Granted, for some people, jogging a half block is a guaranteed to cause extreme gasping for any available oxygen. But the beauty of this kind of activity is that you can pace yourself and increase your stamina—slowly but surely—from one day to the next. Often after just a couple of weeks of a running routine of some kind, you are an entirely new man or new woman vis-à-vis your endurance. So, if you can only handle one-tenth of a mile on day one, do one-tenth of a mile. Try one-eighth of a mile the next day. Before too long, you'll be a candidate for the New York City Marathon—or, at the very least, able to jog a mile without hyperventilating.

18. Creatively Craft from the Comforts of Home

You're temporarily out of work and, for very sound reasons, want to keep idleness to a bare minimum. Making crafts sounds like a fun activity, but you don't want to spend dollars when there's no regular source of income coming in. So, why not get your creative juices flowing with materials that you have lying around the old homestead?

For possibilities in this limitless creative sphere, you might want to check out AllFreeCrafts.com. This website is brimming with crafting ideas that won't cost you one thin dime to initiate. Turn your empty plastic bottles into works of art, as well as your discarded eggshells and yesterday's newspapers. Make a canning jar lamp or wine bottle candleholders. You get the picture.

19. Make a Scrapbook

Scrapbooking, as it's now called, has most definitely assumed a life of its own. In fact, it's fostered something of a cottage industry. Yet, the making of scrapbooks has a rather venerable tradition. It used to be that every young sports fan made a scrapbook consisting of clipped articles from the newspapers, ticket stubs, and assorted memorabilia.

Today, however, scrapbook making is a craft unto itself—a process of recording and preserving your family's life and times. Essentially, it is the preparation of a decorative album of some kind—an attractive and durable scrapbook, if you will—replete with family memories, such as photographs, letters, and snippets of physical reminiscences.

Check out Scrapbooking101.net for some fundamental information on getting started and for additional links on the popular subject. Scrapbooking is certainly a worthy endeavor to kick off during your jobless spell.

20. Practice Some Yoga

In the tongue of ancient India, Sanskrit, *yoga* means *union*. In contemporary times, this union of mind, body, and spirit has given rise to a thriving practice indeed. That is, in all segments of society, the various physical postures and poses that augur mental and spiritual well being are being practiced everywhere from retirement villages to the coldest corporate settings imaginable.

Considering the lack-of-a-job-related stress that you are bearing right now, practicing yoga on a regular basis could prove very helpful. You could do it every day in the comforts of your home and it won't cost you one red cent. For information on this internationally renowned exercise, visit Yoga.com and Yoga.About.com.

Twenty Sites to Sample on the Internet

Describing the Internet as the network of networks
is like calling the Space Shuttle a thing that flies.

—John Lester

When you're certifiably unemployed, the reality of your joblessness stares back at you from every mirror. It looms like a colossus over your daily comings and goings. Fortunately, there's this alternative universe known as *virtual reality*. And while we keep supplying you with websites to call upon for this reason or that reason, we've not, until this moment, furnished you with an eclectic cross-section of Internet addresses to sample. That is, we've yet to unfurl a scintillating mixture of cyber locales with a single binding thread and single binding thread only: They are interesting one and all—if not always enlightening—in some distinctive fashion.

The bottom line is that the websites to follow will engage you on some level outside of the hustle and bustle of your job search. Some of them may stimulate your brain. Others may fascinate you in a way you never dreamed possible. Several of these sites can certainly augment your job safari. By and large, they are listed here as virtual diversions from the life and times of sometimes harried job seekers.

1. Bored.com

For starters, you don't have to be bored silly to pay a call on this website, or, for that matter, any of the others to come. This portal gives you access to everything from amusing witticisms to ridiculous pickup lines to harmless pranks to embarrassing tales from the reality frontier. If it's your bag, you can link from Bored.com to online video games and even generate priceless works of art at your computer desk or on your laptop. Where else on the information superhighway can you compare and contrast your height with the height of your favorite, or not-so-favorite, celebrities? Are you taller than Tom Cruise? Find out the answer at Bored.com.

2. Classmates.com

You've more than likely encountered this Internet business's banner ads in your cyber adventures. While you're sans a source of regular income, why not try to conjure up ghosts from your past? That is, connect with some of the guys and gals in your high school and college graduating classes.

You can become part of the Classmates.com class, as it were, by filling out a basic information form, which, of course, includes your school and year of graduation. This simple act opens up a floodgate of contact possibilities, enabling you to communicate with erstwhile classmates who likewise registered. Classmates.com has a rather sizeable and growing membership. So, do it just to satisfy a curiosity. Do to reconnect with old friends. Do it to expand your network. *Just do it.*

3. TheOnion.com

When life gives you lemons, peel some onions. Or, better yet, visit *The Onion* at TheOnion.com, which bills itself as "America's finest news source." It is only because of *The Onion*'s crack reporting that we learned Oprah just launched her very own reality. Yes, you heard it right—*reality*. *The Onion* is the only news source featuring behind-the-scenes economic stories, such as this one: "Even during tough economic times, the sales outlook for Family Dollar Store continues to be strong, principally because their core business, plastic spiders, has proven recession proof." You just don't get these kinds of scoops in the *Wall Street Journal.*

For the jobless, in particular, this daily news magazine is a must read. Nowhere else will you encounter these kinds of exposés: "Dot-Commers to Receive Unemployment Benefits in Form of Stock Options" and "Thousands Lose Jobs as Michigan Unemployment Offices Close."

4. EBizMBA.com

If you want ready access to the quintessential eBusiness knowledge base, this website is a must stopover. At EBizMBA.com, you'll stumble upon regularly updated lists to the most frequently patronized websites in a panorama of genres, including blogs, politics, health, comedy, celebrities, video games, and more.

5. Heavy.com

While you're out of work and in the thick of the job hunt, you're no doubt doing a lot of—metaphorically speaking—heavy lifting. But this particular heavy lifting—a visit to Heavy.com—is not heavy at all. On the contrary, Heavy.com is a video tour de force, replete with clips in such varied classifications as comedy, animation, news, and animals.

Where else can you watch Bill O'Reilly interview Alf one minute, and then tune in to footage of a three-headed frog in the next breath?

6. CoolSiteOfTheDay.com

Perhaps you begin your days by reading inspirational quotations from one of those ubiquitous 365-day desk calendars. Maybe one of your favorite places is a website featuring a daily dose of encouragement and motivation to take on another day. Well, now it's time to add *entire websites*—a different one every single day—to your daily "of the day" fare.

After painlessly registering with CoolSiteOfTheDay.com, you will receive daily via e-mail the site owner's unscientifically selected cool website of the day. In addition, each and every day on-site, you'll find a word of the day, article of the day, and this day in history. You can't help but leave this place a wiser soul and, logically, more qualified for any job you're seeking.

Unemployment Benefit #14

You have time to initiate a blog and discourse on your adventures and misadventures as a jobless statistic.

7. HowStuffWorks.com

You might as well know all the stuff on this website—things like: What is the average credit score and why? How do wireless powers work? What exactly is pastrami? And how does bounty hunting work? In fact, the latter plays a considerable role in the American justice system and is perfectly legal. Is there a possible career opportunity here?

If nothing else, HowStuffWorks.com supplies its visitors with ample food for thought, along with a veritable encyclopedia of knowledge on subject matters ranging far and wide.

8. JumpTheShark.com

When Arthur Fonzarelli, aka the Fonz, jumped over a penned-in shark while wearing a pair of water skis on the popular sitcom *Happy Days*, a fellow named Jon Hein deemed it a seminal moment in television programming—one, in fact, which all others before it and after it should be judged. Hein subsequently inaugurated an entire website dedicated to a free-flowing discussion of TV shows and the precise moment when they, in effect, ventured far astray from their original concepts—strained credulity, if you will—to bolster declining ratings or, in some instances, to save truly sinking ships. Paying homage to the aforementioned *Happy Days* episode, he christened it JumpTheShark.com.

This site is now a pop-culture phenomenon. And, seeing that you've got a few extra hours to spare on your daily plate, there's no better time than the present for you to drop by and, if you are so inclined, add your unique contribution to the dialogue. That is, select a television show—past or present—that you feel has lost its credibility because of a particular plot twist, abrupt change in actors playing a certain character, or some other peculiarity in production.

9. PointlessSites.com

This website champions itself as the "Premier Portal of Pointlessness." When you're out of work and looking for a job, a little pointlessness goes a long way in reducing stress and, in fact, allowing you to appreciate the more pointed sides of life. PointlessSites.com furnishes you with copious links to sites such as the one dedicated to watching and listening to lambs in real time; to another featuring a "very big pointless list" of global domain names; to still another sporting unique—but pointless—highly magnified images. You can't help but be uplifted by the width and breadth of the pointlessness.

10. MySpace.com

From the pointless to the exceedingly popular MySpace.com we go. If you haven't yet looked into this website, now could be a very opportune time to do so. This interactive social-networking portal in cyberspace is teeming with members sporting detailed personal profiles, photos, and blogs. MySpace.com is an ideal place to network with people who maintain interests similar to yours. This consensus could include like-minded job and career pursuits.

11. Facebook.com

This free-access website is still another popular social network in the virtual ether. If you don't yet know how this site operates, Facebook. com invites its members to join one or multiple networks, which could include, for example, a particular school, a work locale, or a region of the country. In other words, it brings people together based on commonalities, such as attendance at a specific college, a job with a certain company, being a resident of a particular city, and so on. Facebook.com is truly a site for sore jobless eyes.

12. MetaFilter.com

This website is a high activity community weblog. MetaFilter.com permits its members to post their thoughts and their questions for the wider world to see and to comment on.

While you're out of work, you no doubt have more than a few questions rattling around your brain concerning the job and career search. And you just might be interested in what other people have to say regarding them. Hearing first-hand the experiences of others could prove very beneficial to you. Hey, you might be on the receiving end of an invaluable job interview tip. Let's say you're into more thorny matters. Well, you just might learn a new technique to grow more healthy roses.

Whether on-site at MetaFilter.com or pressing the flesh somewhere, make it job one, if you will, to learn from others whenever and wherever you can. And should someone correct you, don't testily bristle and storm off into the night with steam pouring out of your ears. Keep in mind the words of the old proverb: "He that corrects me hands me a gold coin." Have you checked the price of gold lately?

13. InternetSlang.com

Since this section of the book is dedicated to visiting an interesting and rather diverse blend of websites, we'd be remiss if we did not assist you in furthering your Internet vocabulary—or, more appropriately, your Web-speak. InternetSlang.com is your ticket to a virtual blitzkrieg of slang words, acronyms, and abbreviations regularly spotted in the virtual firmament. Did you know that VBG means Very Big Grin; HTH, Hope That Helps; and WFM, Works For Me?

So, don't you concur that visiting this website SLF? No? SCNR.

14. GoAskAlice.Columbia.edu

Since health and wellness issues matter to us now more than ever, you'd be well served by checking into GoAskAlice.Columbia.edu. This website is a popular and highly regarded question and answer forum in the field.

You can, in fact, pose health-related questions of your own here. You can also search the comprehensive site for already addressed answers to questions in every conceivable health and wellness category. From the merely nagging to the potentially life threatening, the responses are plentiful.

On GoAskAlice.Columbia.edu, you can unearth information on everything from the symptoms of colorectal cancer to how to stop snoring to dealing with a stiff back. The bottom line, always, is that you want your jobless mind and body to be functioning at full throttle and working in harmony, and this website can assist you in doing both.

15. MovieLink.com

It is unwise to cast aside your pleasures while serving your unemployment sentence. The key is to stay focused and as stress-free as humanly possible during your jobless days and nights. So, renting a feature film every now and then might be just what the doctor ordered. And why not gain access to it in the form of an immediate download to your PC, TV, or laptop, which you can do at MovieLink.com? This website has all of the popular flicks for rental or outright purchase.

16. TheSmokingGun.com

If you want to see a previously arrested, fingerprinted, and booked celebrity's mug shot, TheSmokingGun.com will more than likely have it stored in the site's growing archives. This website is crawling with government and legal documents acquired via the Freedom of Information Act. In fact, this very real sliver of the rear view of American life and times can assist you in keeping real, while simultaneously providing you with hours of perusing pleasure.

17. RoadsideAmerica.com

While you may not presently be in the financial driver's seat to visit any of the offbeat locales chronicled on RoadsideAmerica.com, you just might want to prepare a list for future consideration—when you are ready, willing, and able to hit the roads again.

RoadsideAmerica.com is overflowing with at once fascinating and unconventional tourist attractions in every region of the country and of every conceivable allure. For instance, there's the Oregon Vortex near Gold Hill, Oregon, where tennis balls seemingly roll uphill and brooms stand on their ends. Do you want to know where America's smallest church buildings are? This website tells you where they are and how big they are, too. If churches aren't your religion, maybe the Baltimore Tattoo Museum is, with its multiple exhibits, innumerable artifacts, and sweeping historical recounting of electric tattooing. Hungry? Well, have you ever eaten in a restaurant with a genuine London double-decker bus parked inside the actual dining room? RoadsideAmerica.com clues you in on where this one-of-a-kind eatery is located, as well as many others with equally curious appeal. It's a website worth cruising through, even if you have no intention of ever traversing the highways and byways to visit a single one of these attractions.

18. BizRate.com

As we've repeatedly noted, one of the fringe benefits of unemployment is free time. Or, more apropos, allotments of time no longer expended in traveling to and from the job and, of course, toiling there for eight, nine, or more hours. So, yes, you've got the time right now to compare and contrast products sold in the Web's top stores. The place to facilitate this informed consumer activism is BizRate.com.

BizRate.com is a consumer's best pal, enabling you to, foremost, harvest a list of choices on the piece of merchandise or service you are considering purchasing. You are then armed with the tools to compare competing manufacturers. That is, you are furnished with information concerning the various products' quality and reliability, as well as customer reviews to give you a clear picture of what actual users are saying. In the final analysis, it's all about getting the best deal, which is always the way to go, most especially when you are absent a full-time job.

19. ThinkExist.com

This website proclaims, "Finding quotes was never this easy." And a visit to ThinkExist.com bears this out. You can search alphabetically for quotations on all kinds of subject matter. Whether you're looking for a little verse to place in your significant other's Valentine's Day card—try L for "Love"—or a clever snippet to quote during a job interview, this website is the place to be. If it's been spoken (or written) *and* deemed worthy of posterity, you'll very likely find it here.

20. FactCheck.org

Our final volley in this surfing contest lands us on the shores of FactCheck.org. Consider this stopover a welcome civics lesson. Founding father John Adams once said, "Facts are stubborn things." And, in the world of politics—where the truth isn't always a prized commodity—we the people desperately need a nonpartisan outfit to vet what our politicians are saying versus the cold, hard facts.

FactCheck.org enables us to be more informed citizens, better prepared to make the right decisions about our leadership. Truth be told, politicians of all stripes impact our lives in very real ways, so it pays to separate the wheat from the chaff. FactCheck.org does yeoman's work in this regard.

Twenty Things You've Been Meaning to Do All These Years

Tomorrow is often the busiest day of the week.

—Spanish proverb

Sure, you've been meaning to do these things and go to these places for an awful long time now. The trouble is that you haven't had ample time or the overwhelming desire to accomplish any of them—at least not yet.

One of the great mysteries of life is that surviving four years of high school often seems like an eternity—more *High School Confidential* than *High School Musical*—while twenty years of adulthood zooms by at warp speed. If one lesson can be extracted from this rather general observation, it's that there's no time like the present to do things and to go places. Naturally, within this to-do/to-go list is locating the right and proper job or career path. But it behooves you to take this current life detour—unemployment—to arenas you've been meaning to play in for a long time.

Since it's not possible for the author to know precisely what you personally have been meaning to do all these years, a little improvising is in order. What follows are some familiar, and some not so common, particulars that folks just like you are always meaning to execute someday.

1. Witness the Rising Sun

This initial entry is an obligatory one for lists of this kind. Clichéd as this may sound, a sunrise is truly something to see live and in person. So, if you've been meaning to experience the aforementioned, set the alarm clock one morning for the appropriate hour (pre-sunrise with sufficient travel time to get where you want to go to witness it unfold in all its splendor).

Actually, experiencing a sunrise in real time is a multilayered affair. That early hour is unlike any later time in the day. It's before the gas-guzzling nation hits the roads. It's prior to the cell-phone nation awakening to place its personal calls in restaurants, argue with significant others while on supermarket checkout lines, and plan daily itineraries while standing at bank ATM machines. And look at it this way: After the sun takes to the sky, the entire day is your oyster. More of a day than you are accustomed to—and more is better.

2. Contact a Long Lost Friend

Many of us have friends from our storied pasts that we've lost touch with altogether. Despite having penned genuine sentiment in school yearbooks to "keep in touch," and exchanged phone numbers and e-mails with departing neighbors and colleagues leaving the job, communication often comes to a screeching halt—it's just the way life works. If you don't know where these people have landed, get out your private investigator accoutrements. Try the aforementioned Classmates. com, MySpace.com, and Facebook.com. Google them. Comb the white pages online. Now you have ready access to phone book listings all across the country.

3. Have Your Portrait Painted by a Street Artist

Okay, so you've always thought about having your portrait painted. But the odds are you're not going to make an appointment with a studio artist and pay big bucks for the privilege, particularly during this parsimonious period in your life. There is, however, an alternative to going down this route. Why don't you sit down with a street artist instead?

You can locate many talented artists plying their trades and showcasing their talents on the sidewalks of big cities, in artsy towns, at street fairs, on boardwalks, and in parks. Even if the process requires you to plop down in front of an artist on a busy thoroughfare, why not go for it? So what if the whole world is watching you for a spell? In the end, it'll be an experience you'll long remember, and you'll have an artist's rendition of you at a most memorable moment in your life—when you're out of a job.

4. Cook a Television Chef's Meal

First, let us feast our eyes on those many TV cooking programs on the airwaves. Kitchen whizzes of all genders, races, nationalities, and personalities prepare domestic and international food dishes spanning the vast cooking spectrum, from appetizers to main courses to desserts. They dazzle and charm audiences day in and day out.

But here's the real kicker: The majority of viewers of these entertaining and instructional cooking shows will never personally attempt any of the featured recipes. A sampling of the more common excuses for not doing so includes not having time, not having the patience, or that the meals are too complex or impractical.

Why then do we watch these shows in such large numbers—and with such enthusiasm—if not for the learned cooking counsel and tempting recipes? There is, after all, a cable network solely devoted to cooking and food programming. The answer may surprise you. Many of us tune in to cooking programs because we find them warm and reassuring on some higher level. We embrace them as soothing respites from life's daily grind. Watching self-assured cooks in action—working their kitchen magic amidst a cornucopia of the foods that we love—is a peaceful stopover. The creative, sometimes exotic, even erotic, but always involved cooking process is elevated to a special place in our hearts, minds, and—yes—eventually in our stomachs, too.

Have you been meaning to cook a recipe or two offered by a small-screen chef? If the answer's yes, it's time to prepare one of Lydia's or Ming's recipes. No more excuses. Use your unemployment moment to stop living vicariously within the cooking experience. Jump into the frying pan! If you need a handy recipe this very minute in black and white, we've got an original and pretty basic one for you. A former professional chef has crafted this recipe solely for this book. It's called Unemployment Tomato Sauce.

Here's what you need:

+ Two tablespoons olive oil
+ One-half medium onion, chopped fine
+ Four cloves garlic, chopped fine
+ Eight to ten plum tomatoes, seeded and coarsely chopped
+ One can tomato sauce
+ One tablespoon tomato paste

+ Pinch clove powder
+ Salt and pepper to taste
+ One bunch fresh basil, chopped

Here's what you do:

1. In a medium pan, heat the oil on medium.
2. Add the onions and garlic. Sweat until tender, approximately five minutes.
3. Add the plum tomatoes. Stir. Cook for five minutes.
4. Add the tomato sauce and paste.
5. Add the clove powder, salt, and pepper.
6. Reduce the heat to a simmer. Cook for twenty minutes.
7. Remove from the heat. Add the fresh basil.

Unemployment Benefit #15

Your nostrils are completely liberated from the stomach-turning aromas of colleagues' fishy lunches heating up in the microwave.

5. Sponsor a Needy Child

You've no doubt seen the poignant commercials importuning you to sponsor a hungry child somewhere in the world for what amounts—annually—to the cost of a daily cup of coffee. And, if you sip your java in a Starbucks, a whole lot less than that. You've maybe felt a yank or two on your heartstrings, but in the end you didn't place that call.

Well, although this may not seem like the best time in your life to be parting with scarce dollars, perhaps it's the ideal time to make such a commitment. Freely giving is always uplifting; giving when you have less to give is even more so. There are many humanitarian outfits that facilitate such sponsorships, including Children International at Children.org and Save the Children at SaveTheChildren.org.

6. Grant a Wish

In a similar vein as sponsoring a child, you may have given some thought to granting the wish of a child with a life-threatening illness. The Make-A-Wish-Foundation at Wish.org is the catalyst that can make this happen. This is your chance to be more than a genie in a bottle. A little generosity on your part goes a long way here.

7. Go Green

Of course, you've probably been meaning to make a considerable contribution to long-term health and wellness of the planet. That is, you've been planning to *go green* in a big way. Kermit the Frog once lamented, "It's not easy being green," but, from where you stand, it's not too hard. In fact, going green can save you green (more than the amount you've committed to sponsoring a needy child or granting the wish of an ill child). There are several rudimentary things you can do to begin accumulating your green credits, including:

✦ Walk or ride a bicycle, where practical, as an alternative to driving a car.

✦ Conserve water whenever and wherever possible. Wash your clothes only when you have a full load. Take shorter showers. Install low-flow showerheads. Attend to leaky faucets. Just be conscious of saving water and you'll save water.

✦ Insulate your home. You'll conserve both energy and dollars this way.

✦ Keep your computer for as long as possible by updating software.

✦ Recycle whatever can be recycled, including yesterday's cell phones.

✦ Install ceiling fans. Run them counterclockwise during the heat of the summer to generate a downdraft; clockwise in the wintertime to more efficiently circulate existing hot air.

✦ Use energy-friendly fluorescent bulbs. The entire continent of Australia is using CFLs (Compact Fluorescent Lamps), so you might as well join the folks from the land down under. Got that, mate?

✦ Don't throw your useable junk in the garbage. Have a yard sale or sell it on eBay.

✦ Plant trees wherever possible. We can never have enough of them.

✦ Carry a reusable tote bag to do your shopping. There's even an entire website devoted to just this kind of thing: ReusableBags. com.

✦ Drink tap water in lieu of the bottled stuff. You are paying mostly for the plastic bottle. One study estimates that 1.5 million barrels of oil per annum is used just to make plastic bottles for water. That's a lot of black gold expended on creating a landfill's worst enemy: the plastic bottle.

8. Fast For a Day

For health or dietary reasons, have you for some time now been mulling over fasting for a day or two? In point of fact, the world's most popular religions—Western and Eastern alike—incorporate instances of fasting into their observances. New Age health and wellness practitioners, too, often sing the praises of brief periods of such dietary abstention to purify the body. The bottom line is that a single day of subsisting on several glasses of water will, if nothing else, test your self-discipline.

9. Balance Your Checkbook

If this has been on your to-do list and you haven't gotten around to it, do it now or forever hold your peace. When you're sans a regular source of income, the last thing you need are bank fees intermittently carpet bombing your checking account. It's not rocket science to know precisely—at any given moment—what is in your checking account. It's basic addition and subtraction, coupled with simple but conscientious bookkeeping.

Making assumptions in this pecuniary bailiwick can augur the aforementioned fee-for-all, including bounced check fees, insufficient funds fees, uncollected funds fees, and so on. And, really, when you're watching every dollar, getting whacked with $25, $30, and charges even higher than that can seem like losing real money. In the big picture, balancing your checkbook gives you control. And the more control you have, the better, particularly when you are between jobs.

10. Prepare Your Last Will and Testament

You said you were going to do it. Legal experts recommend that adults of all ages should have one. So, don't look upon the preparation of a will as macabre or in any way a depressing undertaking. View a last will and testament's crafting as something truly uplifting.

In fact, if you've got such a document, it is written testimony that you have hurdled over two of life's high bars—i.e., you have something to give and someone to give it to. For basic information on putting it all down on paper before you have a proverbial gun to your head, call on AllLaw.com and USLegalForms.com.

11. Throw a Tupperware Party

Admit it, haven't you always wanted to throw a party where you not only serve cheese and crackers, but also make some money between mouthfuls of all the munchies? And, yes, the mother of such gatherings is the vaunted Tupperware party. If this notion has been entangled in your dream catcher, visit Tupperware.com to get the ball rolling. If a Tupperware party doesn't quite pass your macho test—or whatever other test you apply—there are countless commercial epigones that now follow the Tupperware model of house parties.

In fact, you could party on and peddle everything these days from tools to computer software to dog accessories. Maybe a Pupperware party is more up your alley. Invite fellow pet parents to not only eat cake, but also purchase merchandise for their best friends on four legs. To get a feel for what these kinds of parties entail, check out ShurePets.com, a company that christens you a pet consultant and arms you with the necessary trappings of a Pupperware party. And don't forget that these kinds of gatherings—no matter what you are selling—pry open potential doors in your wider job search. Meeting people in festive settings of any stripe is both fun and network-building.

12. Plan a Camping Outing

You've been itching for years to become one with nature—admit it. And, presuming you're not quite up to signing on with a nudist colony, a camping expedition is the more practical option. For too long, you opted for the largesse of the hospitality industry come vacation time. In other words, accommodations with, at the bare minimum, swimming pools and wireless Internet.

Why not experience a swimming hole and no cyber hopping, at least for a few days? After all, you're not on vacation now—you're a verifiable jobless statistic. Rough it for a spell in the wilds! Bring the first aid kit and mosquito repellant and you're good to go. If you need help locating a camping hotspot—or cold spot, if it's wintertime—try Camping.com, which is an information bonanza on the subject at hand.

13. Rent Those Cinema Classics

Citizen Kane's been on your must-watch movie list for how long now? Sure, you've heard it referred to as the greatest movie ever made. And yes, you've planned on renting it time and again, but opted for such safe bets as *13 Going on 30* and *Scary Movie* instead. "Next time," you said.

Well, why not make next time right now? Take this extraordinary parcel of time in your life to break out the popcorn and watch the flicks that the movie buffs can't stop praising. Find out once and for all what all the fuss is about. And while film aficionados may disagree on what pictures should grace the top-five list, this modest book has arrived at a carefully calibrated consensus:

1. *Citizen Kane*
2. *Casablanca*
3. *Lawrence of Arabia*
4. *The Godfather*
5. *Gone With the Wind*

14. Join a Group

You've long been meaning to join the Joiner Family. That is, you've always wanted to be part of a group. You've wanted to go on record as supporting causes dear to your heart. Maybe it's a certain political issue that's long been your passion. Has picketing been an enduring aspiration of yours? Perhaps it's an environmental cause that's been stirring in your insides. Have you long wanted to lie down in front of a bulldozer? Does wearing retro clothes and re-enacting battles of past wars paint the picture of your lasting fantasy?

Whatever are your singular interests and special fervor, there are like-minded individuals who share them—groups of people dedicated to the same causes, beliefs, or interests. Whether you want to save Darfur or leap into frigid ocean waters, there's surely a group or well-established society for you to join. And, for certain, you'll be a better person for having done so. A future career might just be the offspring of the Joiner Family, too—you never know. Make a contribution to the fight—whatever your preferred fight happens to be.

15. Write a Personal Mission Statement

Since this is the twenty-first century, you've probably been yearning to develop a personal mission statement to guide you, not only in your job and career search, but also in keeping your life on an even keel. A mission statement is essentially a goal or set of goals. It's where you want to end up in your personal relationships, career endeavors, lifestyle, and contributions to the society at large. Look upon your mission statement as a pithy description of how you would like to be remembered—your legacy.

There are no rules or set formulae in preparing a mission statement. It could be a couple of sentences or a couple of pages long. Sure, it's generally better to be succinct. But in the final analysis, you should enunciate what you want to achieve in life. The harder part is setting out to achieve it.

16. Paint Your Living Quarters

Oh, yes, this room and that room in your humble quarters could use a fresh coat of paint and something of a makeover. A painting adventure on your part could bear some sweet fruit. Foremost, your surroundings will look cleaner, brighter, and cheerier when newly painted. So, from an aesthetic perspective you're ahead of the game right away. But, in addition to appearance, it's plainly better to operate from a home base that is tidy and unsoiled. It'll help ensure that your job search is also tidy and unsoiled. Fresh paint can be a nice depression deflector, too.

17. Wash Your Windows

Depending on exactly where you call home, this particular task may be your sole responsibility or the responsibility of a building maintenance crew. Nevertheless, it's almost always up to you to clean the insides of your windows. If you're living on the thirtieth floor of an apartment complex, one wouldn't expect you to crawl along the outside window ledges to wash them.

Regardless of what your particular responsibility is in this area, you know that a serious cleaning of your windows has been on your agenda for some time now. It's important at this point in your life—and, really, in all points of your life—to see clearly. And clean windows can go a long way in enabling you to see the forest for the trees. This is a window of opportunity that should not be passed up.

18. Go Skydiving

This is definitely one of life's more high-flying escapades. Many of us have skydiving on our to-do lists. At least, those of us who are not afraid of heights and have a real thirst for adventure. It's also fitting that a prior entry in this chapter is the composition of your last will and testament.

Fear not! Skydiving is a rather safe affair, provided you have a parachute. You can call on SkyDiving.com (1-800-493-JUMP) and DropZone.com for a sky full of information on this potentially exhilarating pursuit.

19. Become a Street Performer

If you have ample doses of courage, confidence, and self-respect—not to mention a modicum of talent in the entertainment arena—you've probably been meaning to take to the streets and showcase your particular genius as a street performer. For information on this unique brand of public performance, check out Performers.net.

Worth noting here is that in most locales of the country, a street performer permit is required before any lights, camera, action can legally transpire in the great outdoors. So, if you're anything from a gifted guitarist to a proficient mime, consider the possibilities of street performing, and don't forget to pass around the hat.

Unemployment Benefit #16

You can give yourself your very own performance reviews.

20. Invent Something

Hey, if you've been tinkering around in your garage, or on your kitchen table, inventing the next must-have piece of merchandise, why not take it to the next level? You've been meaning to for a long time now. If this scenario fits your profile, consider getting a patent for your idea. The United States Patent and Trade Office at USPTO.gov (1-800-786-9199) will furnish you with all the particulars.

Inventing a sellable product is hardly the sole province of Mensa members fiddling around with test tubes in laboratories and uber-thick-glasses-wearing computer geeks. Ordinary people like you invent stuff that finds its way into the marketplace every single day. So, you've created a one-of-a-kind cat toy that has passed the fussy feline test—i.e., your furry friend loves it. Well, get it out of your house and into the hands of consumers. If you're serious and advanced in the invention game, you might want to check out InventionHome.com. This company is staffed by inventors, for inventors and can show you how to transform your budding idea into a finished product selling on store shelves.

Twenty Ways to Avoid Becoming Antisocial

You essentially will have to "socialize" your way into a network.

—Travis Kalanick

Unfortunately, modern society has made being an antisocial lump a rather effortless affair. When you can accomplish virtually everything at your computer (shopping, paying bills, applying for jobs), it definitely makes being a social butterfly all the more challenging—something, in fact, that you've got to really work at. Nowadays, there are just too many tasks we can perform without interfacing with genuine flesh-and-blood human beings. And nowhere does the specter of antisocial actions and inactions loom larger than in the hearts and minds of the unemployed.

Throughout this book, we've touched upon many of the antisocial themes that arise when you are out of a job. You know the score by now. Suddenly, and without much warning, you don't have to get up and go to work in the morning. And, if you so desire, you can stay in bed pretty much all day, click on the television set and simultaneously surf the Internet on your laptop. Theoretically, you could spend the preponderance of your day with a bowl of potato chips at your side and the aforementioned laptop on your stomach. When you absolutely must venture outside, you could get all the cash you need from an ATM machine and pay for your groceries at a self-checkout. Let's face it—the scenario just laid out isn't exactly a recipe for healthy social behavior.

So much has already been said on these pages concerning the sheer importance of interacting with fellow human beings. Get out into the wide-open spaces, and don't succumb to lethargy, isolation, and, worst of all, depression. Sure, we keep importuning you to visit this website and that website. And each and every one is worth calling on. Of course you should apply for jobs online. You should also extensively research job and career opportunities on the Internet. There's nothing wrong with having a grand old time in the virtual ether. But this isn't to imply that you should become a wholly preoccupied life form that stalks cyberspace at the expense of socializing with your fellow human animals. No, there's ample room for both utilizing the Web to its utmost potential and for consistently commingling with your two-legged brethren. There is nothing gained in becoming a recluse.

Here is a sampling of suggestions—to add to what has already been enunciated on this critical topic—which will ensure that you never lose sight of the fact that you are part and parcel of the very social species known as *Homo sapien*:

1. Stay Clean

At this precise moment in your life and times, you'd be wise to stay clean. Yes, keep out of trouble and don't neglect your overall hygiene.

Even if not having a job necessitates the cutting back on expenses, things like soap, toothpaste, deodorant, and shampoo should be spared the full wrath of your budget ax (although you can, naturally, shop for bargains on these sanitary products).

Sitting atop the social behavior pyramid is cleanliness. It is, after all, next to godliness. You can never go wrong by remaining groomed and foul odor–free during your joblessness. It'll not only aid and abet you in the job search, but enable you to be more social and win people over to your side. Dandruff, halitosis, and body odor are public enemies number one, two, and three when it comes to hitting the social bull's-eye.

2. Say Hello

Depending on where the postman delivers your mail, the common courtesy of saying hello to passersby or neighbors may or may not be in vogue. In New York City, for instance, nodding your head to a stranger—or God forbid, uttering an outright salutation—is often interpreted as a threatening act, something akin to a cat raising its back. Nevertheless, there are appropriate times and appropriate people who merit a hello or some sort of acknowledgement from you—even on the impersonal streets of thriving metropolises.

This advice comes straight out the Social Behavior 101 lesson plan. A simple greeting to somebody you don't know, or don't know very well, can open doors. You might be living next door to the guy who has the in to get you your dream job. But you've got to know who he is and what he does before this can happen.

3. Tune in to the World

There's plenty of time in the day for you to tune in to your favorite music selections or listen to the twenty-four-hour news station. You needn't walk the streets with your iPod or MP3 player at maximum volume. Filling your ears with mega-decibels and cutting yourself off entirely from what's going on all around you is not exactly conducive to social interaction.

If being more social is your larger goal, this mode of behavior—as the rule rather than the exception when you're out in public—is a very bad habit to call your own. And, on top of everything else, plugging your ears with unceasing sound while strolling the highways and byways increases your chances of being struck by a bus or ice cream truck. And, courtesy of your antisocial behavior, you'll never know what hit you.

4. Keep Abreast of Current Events

In order to be a truly social animal in good standing, you've got to be something of a conversationalist. And this, in many instances, requires that you have a modicum of awareness of what's happening in the world in which you live. Read the daily newspapers and watch the nightly news programs. Keep abreast, too, of whom Simon Cowell has just insulted, who's who on *Survivor*, and what Rickrolling means, as well as the trials and tribulations of Paris Hilton and Britney Spears.

5. Listen to Others

In addition to being capable of intelligently conversing with your fellow men and women, it behooves you also to be a good listener. This trait alone will put you ahead of the class, since so many people—sad to say—would rather talk ad nauseum about themselves than listen to a word you, or anybody else, has to say.

You know who they are. No matter what's transpiring in your life, it's always about them. You mention that you lost your job. They respond, "Oh, when I lost my job . . ." Don't be like these self-absorbed, supercilious bags of hot air. Just listen to others—be interested in them—and they, in turn, will want to listen to you.

6. Chat with the Neighbors

Unless you live on a family farm in Iowa corn country, or a cattle ranch in the badlands of North Dakota, more than likely you've got a few neighbors within shouting distance. Nevertheless, few would not argue that it's a colder, more impersonal world that we live in than, say, fifty years ago. Courtesy of the snowballing advances in technology, ease of communication, and multiple media alternatives, this huge planet has also shrunk in size. The irony is that within the intimacy ushered in by the Information Age, living and breathing people have been pushed further and further apart.

In other words, you can live next door to some people and rarely, if ever, see them. You can have next-door neighbors—sometimes for many years—and not know a thing about them. But these kinds of relationships—or, more aptly, lack of relationships—are not preordained by the law of the times. Even in the frosty new millennium, you can get to know your neighbors—most of them anyway—by first saying hello and, if it feels right, eventually initiating conversation. Countless folks are shocked when they discover how much they have in common with their formerly faceless neighbors and now close personal friends.

7. Patronize Yard Sales

Attending yard sales—or garage or house sales, it doesn't matter— is an excellent adventure vis-à-vis maintaining social contact with the wider world. And, on top of that, you can pick up some real bargains along the way. You meet and greet people—often your neighbors—and unearth low-priced goodies, which could come in handy while you're out of work and watching your pennies.

In a similar vein—and we've mentioned it earlier in the book—you could run one of these sales yourself. This is an outstanding route to venture down both to ward off antisocial demons and bring in a few welcome bucks.

8. Be Spontaneous

Filter your tap water if you like, but not every single word that comes out of your mouth or everything you write in your e-mails. This is not a suggestion to be profane or insulting. Continue to scrupulously filter out that sort of thing in your socialization campaign! Rather, it's asking that you be more real and not perpetually worried about how you are being perceived.

The bottom line is that you don't want to sound like a telemarketer or used car salesman when you're talking with your fellow men and women. Being continuously image-conscious won't help you make friends, have fun, or grow your network. You needn't overanalyze what to say before cutting loose. Be yourself.

Unemployment Benefit #17

You are emancipated to apportion as much time as you choose to the wearing of your birthday suit.

9. Exercise with Friends

To nip any antisocial tendencies in the bud, there's nothing quite like a little activity in the company of others. Exercising, for example, can be engaged in either alone or alongside your fellow man or woman. And since this chapter is all about commingling with your peers in the human race, we're more interested here in the communal brand of exercising.

Why not go walking or running with a friend or friends? Get a group together and play basketball, volleyball, or whatever ball suits your fancy. Take the tennis racket out of mothballs and find both a partner and a court. Not only are these very social affairs, but any such activities are also a boon for your physical health and wellness.

10. Attend Community Meetings

No matter where you live—a congested city, leafy suburb, or sleepy small town—there are issues big and small that can greatly impact your everyday life. There are also community-related meetings to attend, where you can speak your piece and throw your weight around. The bottom line is that being active in community affairs is a great way to see your neighbors, as well as make a real difference in your life and, in fact, the lives of others.

Don't forget that your presence at community issue gatherings often places you in the same room as the movers and shakers in your little part of the world. When you're out of work, it can only help to ramp up this kind of interaction—and, for that matter, just about every other kind of interaction—because making more and more contacts casts your job net into more and more promising waters.

11. Sit at a Diner Counter

If you're in need of a quick social fix, you could do a whole lot worse than sitting at the counter of your favorite diner or, perhaps, patronizing one for the first time. This, after all, is a longstanding and respected American tradition.

Visualize this: You're sitting on a stool and closely interacting with both those who serve and those who dine. In addition to the obvious sociability boon inherent in this eating milieu, you simultaneously get to feast your eyes on lemon meringue and cherry pies, along with platters of Jell-O and rice pudding. And since you're more than likely monitoring your money situation closely these days—and maybe your calories, too—you don't even have to make these social adventures full dining affairs. You could merely sip a cup of coffee—or Lemon Zinger tea—when there. Just be sure to converse with one and all in the diverse and always opinionated community of diner people.

12. Chew Off a Bartender's Ear

Yes, it's perfectly acceptable for you to chew off a bartender's ear every now and then. Of course, this mastication is metaphorical and should not to be taken literally. But, literally speaking, it's a bartender's job to chitchat and, when appropriate, commiserate with the clientele in addition to preparing and serving assorted spirits.

Now, you don't have to go on any lost weekends, as it were, to tread upon this oft-frequented social arena. And depending on your distinct personality, you've got every imaginable choice as to what kind of bar and what kind of bartender you choose to haunt. Keep in mind, too, that bartenders will not only lend you their ears, but they are renowned for having their ears to the ground, so to speak, and know an awful lot of people, including the very folks who can assist you in locating the right job or career path. Bartenders serve all kinds of people, talk with them, and—in some instances—innocently listen in on their cell phone conversations. In other words, they know what's going down.

A worthwhile footnote here is the notion of bartending as a career or part-time position. For more information on the discipline, visit the quintessential online community for bartenders at Bartending.com. You'll encounter links to bartending schools, job openings, and tips and tools of the trade.

13. Run with the Dogs

If you are among the vast number of American households who count a canine member in the family census, you've got a hot ticket to the wider world's social life. And no, this isn't about socializing with your furry friend, which is admittedly admirable and a whole lot of fun; it's about translating your obvious devotion to the four-legged into some serious socializing with your own kind.

In other words, you can employ your canine companion to meet new friends—or, at the very least, new acquaintances. It's rather simple: Bring your pooch to a nearby dog run. When given the opportunity, most dogs relish cavorting with their own species for a spell. And, at the same time, you get a chance to kibitz with fellow dog lovers, who, most auspiciously, just happen to be human beings. This is a win-win socializing situation for both the human animal and the animal animal.

14. Join a Club

Following up on your summit with fellow dog parents (assuming you fit into this demographic), there are countless clubs and get-togethers that exist all across the fruited plain. People who share a common bond—a certain passion, special interest, or particular talent—convene on a recurrent basis.

Indeed, there are established clubs that run a wide gamut from love of a distinct dog breed to cat breed to domesticated bird. There are clubs devoted to hobbies in everything from stamp collecting to bird-watching to crocheting. There are clubs that meet on issues of importance to their local communities. Seek and you shall find! And, again, the more people that you encounter on a repeated basis, the bigger your network and the spread of its tentacles.

15. Accept Party Invitations

So, you're out of a job. "No job? No prob!" This is hardly the time for you to ensconce yourself in a bedroom bunker. It's also not a particularly propitious time for you to be declining party invitations.

Since the majority of the working population has been, is, or will someday be unemployed during their income-earning years, there's nothing to be ashamed of in being temporarily absent a paying job. And, need we say it again, parties with friends and others keep you out there—social and active—and simultaneously reinforce your network. Have a blast and increase your chances of landing a good job; it's a powerful combo.

16. Throw a Party

You can attend parties as a guest, but you also can throw a party or two. Invite friends and friends of friends. Socialize. Mingle. Speak candidly about your current circumstances.

Let the word go forth that you're looking for a new job or change of careers. Make it known exactly what you've got in mind and what you anticipate in remuneration. The more people who see you and converse with you, the better. It's nice to have as many spotters as possible out and about helping you find a job. And, let's face it, it's always a good feeling to throw a party and uncork a few bottles, including, most of all, your bottled up emotions. Worried about an excessive outlay of dollars? Make it a potluck dinner party.

17. Join a Health Club

If you can afford this small luxury right now, it's a worthy investment and an idyllic avenue to venture down to ensure that you maintain social contacts with living and breathing—or, in this instance, sweating and panting—fellow human travelers. In the process, you remain active and in tip-top physical shape—two accomplishments that truly matter, most especially after you've been knocked for one of life's infamous loops.

18. Join a Book Club at the Local Library

There are, in fact, library book clubs in virtually every nook and cranny of the country. These clubs provide great opportunities for you to at once socialize with your neighbors and stimulate your brain.

Unemployment Benefit #18

By the bright light of day, you can finally match the surnames on your neighbors' mailboxes with their smiling and, in some cases, scowling faces.

19. Take a Craft Class

We all have special talents and aptitudes. But sometimes they require a little nurturing to rise to the surface and to flourish. This reality is precisely why there are craft classes and frequent workshops offered at local community centers, churches, and other locales. Pay close attention to what's happening around you. Look for available classes on subject matter of particular interest to you.

If you've got a latent talent, it's time to let it see the bright light of day. Meet people in the process. You never know where this kind of thing could lead. In any event, attending crafting classes of whatever kind can only augur positive things for your future. When you both socialize and showcase your talents, it's a neat one-two punch.

20. Choose People Over Machines

Consider the final entry in this section as something of a summary of all that's been said. That is, if you are concerned about slipping and sliding into hermit standing, it would be prudent for you to choose interacting with people over impersonal machines when there is a choice.

In other words, stand on line in the bank and interact with a teller instead of punching a keyboard and screen at an ATM machine. Fill up your gas tank at a full-service station—if, of course, the price is right. Speak with a live operator on the telephone rather than pushing one or two, and one or two again, for fifteen minutes leading to nowhere. Pay for your groceries at a checkout stationed by someone on the store's payroll. When you can and where you can, seek out people and human contact.

Ten Things to Do with Your Old Briefcase

Me carrying a briefcase is like a hot dog wearing earrings.
—Sparky Anderson, legendary baseball manager

So, exactly what are you planning to do with that old briefcase of yours? You know, the one that you carted back and forth—day after day, week after week, and month after month—to the office you once upon a time called home. Well, it's time to make a clean break from your employment past and recycle that thingamajig—that unwanted relic from yesteryear. Here is a potpourri of possibilities on how to accomplish exactly that.

1. Make a Time Capsule

Prepare a time capsule for subsequent generations to discover and thumb through. Use your old briefcase to house mementoes from today. Once it's crammed with what you want posterity to know about you and the world you live in, bury it somewhere. Make it a spot where someone in the next century will likely discover and dig up the briefcase. That is, not a spot for raccoons to discover and dig it up the day after tomorrow.

2. Bronze It

You know how some parents get their youngsters' first baby shoes bronzed as permanent keepsakes and reminders of their little ones when they were as precious as precious can be? Well, as a testament to what once was and, more importantly, your tenacity to move on to Act II, you could do the very same thing with your briefcase.

3. Convert It Into a Flowerpot

If your former briefcase is more of an attaché case than leather or otherwise soft, it could make a neat flowerpot. You often see unusual flowerpots in shapes of everything from animals to the buck-naked on two legs. So, a briefcase flowerpot would fit in nicely. Keep in mind that you'll have to punch out a few holes in the bottom to facilitate proper water drainage.

4. Make an At-Home Safe Deposit Box

If you want a safe deposit box in the comforts of home, sweet home, then by all means covert your erstwhile briefcase into a repository of some of the valuables lying around your living space. Then, of course, hide it in a hard-to-find spot, or it wouldn't qualify as much of a safe deposit box.

5. Formulate a Treasure Map

How about devising a clever treasure map leading prospective treasure hunters to a mysterious valuable or valuables? Place the treasure map in that surplus briefcase of yours and leave it where someone will undoubtedly find it and be inspired to rummage through it. Of course, you've got to have a valuable piece of some sort, with which you are willing to part, buried or otherwise hidden somewhere. You wouldn't want to lead anybody on a wild goose chase.

6. Store Your Financial Records

Briefcases and financial records go together like pizza with pepperoni and Chinese takeout with duck sauce. Store your past tax returns, bank statements, stock certificates (if you've got them), bonds (ditto)—the whole kit and caboodle—in your bygone briefcase. Having all of these documents safely ensconced in one place—and with a carrying handle to boot—is a winning idea.

7. Transform It Into a Wishing Well

Put your old briefcase in the closet and pull it out when you've got a wish to make or goal to espouse. Write the said wish or goal down on paper and place it in the briefcase. After a period of time (to be determined by you), check out what you've been wishing for and whether you're realizing your goals. Then, determine if that old briefcase of yours is functioning well (or not) as a wishing well. If it's the latter, see the other nine suggestions in this chapter for a Plan B.

8. Create a Road Safety Kit

Put that briefcase of yours in the trunk of your car and fill it up with roadside safety accoutrements, such as a flashlight and flat tire fixer.

9. Convert It Into a Magazine Rack

Considering all the stuff that's sold as newspaper and magazine racks these days in Bed, Bath & Beyond and its competitors, your retired briefcase would do the job nicely and probably go with your décor, too.

10. Make a Recycling Bin

Depending on where you live, and what you have to recycle—as well as what your former briefcase is made of—you might have a tailor-made recycling bin in your possession. Store your accumulating newspapers and magazines in it until recycling pickup day, or when you're ready to make that trip to the local landfill.

Ten Ways to Modify Your Old Work Clothes

Every new beginning comes from some other beginning's end.

—Seneca, ancient Roman philosopher

Okay, now that you've put your briefcase out to pasture, it's time to do the very same with your erstwhile work duds. Convert your former employment attire into something useful in the here and now. Here's an assortment of ideas on what to do with those retired threads:

1. Make a Patchwork Quilt

If you've got a knack for sewing, you could make a quilt from various snippets of your old work clothes. If you can't sew a lick, partner with someone who can. Patchwork quilts are sometimes about telling stories, with each patch coming from a different place or article of clothing. No doubt, your various work duds tell a rather full and layered story.

2. Use Them as Painting Clothes

If you are planning any paint jobs, or extensive household cleaning chores, it's always prudent to wear old clothes. Your former job wardrobe now makes the grade.

3. Give Them to a Needy Scarecrow

Who says that scarecrows should only wear old flannel shirts and tattered jeans? Dress your scarecrow for success. Clothes make the scarecrow.

4. Make Halloween Decorations Out of Them

Halloween has assumed a whole new dimension in recent years. More and more people are decorating their homes and going to parties in the spirit of the holiday, not unlike Christmastime. There are countless out-of-the-ordinary and bloodcurdling creatures you could make from your surplus clothing line. Witches, ghosts, goblins, and jack-o'-lanterns are always in need of a few good garments.

5. Nifty Clothes Make Nifty Rags

Where is it written that only old socks and T-shirts can be employed as rags? Your old work clothes would definitely kick your rag bag up a notch.

6. Make a Voodoo Doll

Perhaps you've always wanted to stick a few pins in your ex-boss or a backbiting former colleague. Since the law does not permit such barbarism, you could play it safe and legal by making a voodoo doll from snippets of your old work clothes. And, if this endeavor serves as a cleansing catharsis—and stress buster—you could always crank up the assembly line and exorcise a few more demons.

Unemployment Benefit #19

You are free from the sight and sound of a neighboring colleague running his electric razor across his face every ten minutes to—one can only surmise—stave off three, four, and five o'clock shadows.

7. Fly a Decorative Flag

Decorative flags of all sorts—seasonal, sports teams, foreign nations—are very popular in retail shops these days. So, why not make a flag out of your former work clothes and let it rip in the wind?

8. Make a Rope

You've probably always wanted to know how strong a rope could be made by tying together multiple articles of clothing. Through the years in movies and on televisions shows, you've likely witnessed countless people make their escapes from upper-floor apartments and office buildings by shimmying down clothes ropes. Well, while this daring act isn't recommended, making a clothes rope out of your old work wardrobe is. It is, after all, always a good thing to have a rope around. You never know when you might need one. If, for instance, you catch a burglar, you could tie him up with the clothes rope.

9. Shred Your Work Apparel Into Pillow Stuffing

Take all of your old work clothing and cut it up into hundreds of pieces to make stuffing. No, not the Thanksgiving dinner kind, but for pillows and whatever else could use a little fabric filling.

10. Use Your Retired Duds as Shower Mats

Look upon modifying your work clothes as a clean break from one complete chapter in your life. And what could be a cleaner duty than employing them as shower mats and drying your clean two feet on them?

Ten Home Redecorating Ideas You Can Accomplish Free of Charge

Donkey: Whoa. Look at that. Who'd wanna live in a place like that?
Shrek: That would be my home.
Donkey: Oh, and it is lovely. You know, you're really quite a decorator.
It's amazing what you've done with such a modest budget.
I like that boulder. That is a nice boulder.

—*Shrek* (2001)

When you're out of a job and spending more time than ever keeping the home fires burning, it's an opportune moment to do a little redecorating and spruce up your living quarters. So, working with the premise that you don't have a home redecorating budget to draw from, the following suggestions won't cost you an arm and leg. In fact, they won't trigger one single debit from your net worth.

1. Eliminate Clutter

For starters, eliminating clutter in your humble abode should be job one in your home redecoration efforts. It won't cost you a penny to get rid of unnecessary or extraneous stuff in your space. You can even make some money in this redecorating arena by selling your surplus clutter in a yard sale or on eBay. If you choose, you could donate it all to charity.

Unemployment Benefit #20

The only dirty dishes you need look upon are your own, not those of some inconsiderate slob who works alongside you.

2. Rearrange Your Furniture

Here's another suggestion that won't cost you anything—except perhaps a sore back. Move your various pieces of furniture around. It's a brand new look that you can achieve with all of the same things. Rearrange the location of your couch, bed, bookshelves, and coffee table to different geographic locations in their respective rooms. In the end, you might just discover that you have more room in your rooms.

3. Display Your Library of Books

You've quite likely accumulated a few books in your various travels. Perhaps it's time to display them for the entire world to see. Place them strategically on the coffee table or on wall shelves in the living room. Books make for good conversation pieces, too, which will no doubt benefit you as host of the multiple parties you'll be throwing in the future.

4. Display Your Photographs

Tell your story in pictures and decorate your surroundings with the visual images of your life and times. Make a photo gallery. Just as with the visual display of books, photographs of you and yours are sure to spark some interest and subsequent banter from your houseguests.

5. Display a Basket of Fresh Fruit

And you thought only television families had fruit bowls with edible fruit sitting atop coffee tables in their living rooms. Well, the reality is that it isn't just the province of fictional folks on the small screen. You can do it, too. Of course, while fresh fruit makes for an appealing picture, it won't stay that way in perpetuity. In fact, it won't look that way for more than a couple of days. You've got to periodically eat the fruits of this redecorating labor and replenish them, or you run the risk of having a rotting and stinking mess on display.

6. Show Off Your Collection

If you collect something, don't squirrel away the particulars in boxes and stuff it all in closets. What's the point? Devise appropriate displays of your collectibles and decorate your home with the objects of your special passion.

7. Display Your Own Artwork or Craft

If you have an artistic talent, showcase it on your walls (paintings, for instance) or on your bookshelves, tables, wall units, and credenzas (your craft creations, for example). Artwork merits being seen by the wider world, or, at the very least, visitors to your humble abode.

8. Decorate with Live Plants

Although this suggestion could cost you a nominal sum, there is a way to get around even that small outlay of dollars. First of all, you can decorate your home with a nice touch of living by bringing in houseplants and properly tending to their upkeep. To paint your thumb green and not spend any green, throw a house redecorating party with a theme: houseplants.

9. Scrub Your Walls

If you don't want to pick up a paintbrush and plunk down bucks on expensive paints, why don't you just give your walls a thorough scrubbing? You might just discover that it's almost as good as a fresh coat of paint.

10. Wash Your Walls with the Light of the Day

Do you realize that by merely allowing more of the natural light of day into your living space, you've accomplished a bit of redecorating? In fact, free light can dramatically alter the look of your surroundings. You could smoothly affect this redecorating measure by changing the colors of your drapes and curtains (dark to light) or the lengths and heights of the aforementioned. Just pulling up your blinds during the daylight hours could also do the trick.

CHAPTER

TWELVE

Twenty Ways to Get Smarter

None of us are as smart as all of us.

—Japanese Proverb

U p until this point in the book, you've been supplied with a rather diverse mixture of ideas and suggestions on things you can do with your newfound and, alas, temporary free time. You've been furnished with copious job search tips and tools. Some very fertile regions to forage in for both immediate part-time work and potential long-term careers have also been revealed. And you've certainly been given more than a few nudges to visit a wide assortment of websites to assist you in doing everything from saving serious money to experiencing hearty laughs to, of course, finding fulfilling work.

So, in practical reality, you've been gradually padding your smarts as you plow through these pages and take full advantage of the abundant information and resources at your disposal. But in the smart game, there are no time-outs. What follows are twenty encapsulated possibilities to serve as a convenient get-smart blueprint.

1. Keep Your Learning Curve Perpetually Greased

Further your education any way you can. If there are available courses or workshops at nearby colleges or elsewhere, attend them when the subject matter interests you. Would an advanced college degree in your field, or a degree in another discipline entirely, benefit your present job search or, perhaps, inspire a future career? Look into the many possibilities available to advance your formal education, even the cyberspace pathways. The University of Phoenix at Phoenix.edu (1-866-766-0766), for example, is an institution of higher learning that offers various degree programs that can be completed entirely online.

2. Enhance Your Written Communication Skills

If there is one deficiency that stands out like the proverbial sore thumb in the contemporary labor market, it's the dearth of communication skills that manifestly exists in the job pool at large. In particular, written communication is something of a lost art in the age of the sentence fragment, non-punctuated e-mails, and—even lower still on the communication scale—text messaging.

How do you better yourself in this key communication sphere? For starters, read more and write more. But also make a good faith effort to communicate more intelligently in everything you do. For instance, when composing e-mail, capitalize the first letter of the first word in a sentence. End your sentences with periods. Is that too much to ask? For some free counsel on written communication aptitudes, as well as information on problem solving, time management, stress management, and leadership skills, call on MindTools.com, a website that heralds "Essential Skills for an Excellent Career."

Unemployment Benefit #21

You are out of earshot of the perpetual personal phone conversations of some of the most supercilious twits on planet Earth.

3. Read the Dailies Daily

Utilize the print dailies in your neck of the woods to help you find your next job, but also to keep you abreast of what's happening in both your community and the wider world around you. Make use of online newspapers, too. If you want to locate newspapers that are also available in cyberspace, sample OnlineNewspapers.com. This portal enables you to unearth newspapers all over the country and, indeed, the world, that maintain online presences.

4. Keep an Open Mind Open for Business

Unfortunately, modern education sometimes seems intent on inculcating students with a murky, feel-good, one-way-street mode of thinking. But there are infinite gray areas in the game of life. There are honest differences of opinion on many topics and the contentious issues of the day. Keep in mind that not everybody who disagrees with you is a naïf or, worse still, the personification of evil. Respect others with different worldviews than your own and you will be, by osmosis, smarter for having done so.

5. Keep a Dictionary Handy

Not only is it a good idea to read books on as many subjects as possible, but it's also a smart idea to keep a dictionary nearby when doing so. Look up the definitions of unfamiliar words. If your dictionary is the World Wide Web, you should count Dictionary.com among your favorite places. Not only can you procure the definitions you need to augment your vocabulary inventory at this website, but you can also sign up for a daily free word, which will arrive in your e-mail box every morning.

Unemployment Benefit #22

With a little extra time on your hands, you can impress (or disgust) family and friends by learning the names of all the U.S. presidents in chronological order.

6. Be Your Own Consumer Advocate

In these times of breathtaking economic uncertainty coupled with a humongous consumer marketplace, it behooves you to know precisely what your money is buying. As an educated consumer, your life can be greatly enhanced on multiple levels. Foremost, you'll get the best bang for your buck. But you'll also get quality that you can rely on.

To assist you in your education, read *Consumer Reports* magazine or visit their website at ConsumerReports.org. You'll encounter ratings and recommendations in such areas as appliances, babies and kids, cars, electronics, food, home and garden, and money (investments). Also, wade through Epinions.com, a place where consumers just like you have their say. Indeed, people speak their pieces and discourse on their experiences with products and services that run the gamut from DVD players to travel hotspots to frothy beers.

7. Cavort with Genuinely Successful People

First of all, whom you deem a successful person is entirely your call. This is a subjective business. These days, way too much emphasis is placed on the size of an individual's bank account. For countless men and women, money is, in fact, a synonym for success. And, yes, one can be truly successful with a net worth the size of Rhode Island. But a person with the very same wealth can also be an empty-headed oaf devoid of heart and soul.

The bottom line is that you want to find truly successful people—good to the core—who neatly blend the best qualities of humanity. Bring these caliber folks into your network, talk to them, learn from them, and, hopefully, become lasting friends with them.

8. Go to the Head of the Class

You've been importuned earlier in the book to take full advantage of your local libraries. That said, you should also patronize the big daddy of all libraries: the Library of Congress at LOC.gov. Did you know that this library leviathan maintains 532 miles of shelves chock full of materials? This resource paradise also sports a vast and increasing digital collection, which includes films, interviews, pictures, and historical documents.

9. Don't Ignore All Our Yesterdays

In *The History of the Peloponnesian War*, Thucydides said, "History is philosophy teaching by examples." Yes, read about the past. Watch programming on the History Channel and other networks that highlight all that came before us. Visit TheHistoryNet.com, the website of the planet's leading history magazine publisher.

10. Keep a Mistake Log

Journal writing is a noble endeavor that is rich in benefits. It helps you express yourself and enhances your written communication skills. Putting your thoughts and feelings on paper often serves as a welcome emotional purge, too. And, last but not least, a journal is a historical record of your life and times.

In addition to maintaining a traditional journal, you might also want to keep a mistake log, as it were. Write down, as they occur, what you deem to be your mistakes. This act of physically recording them enables you to clearly identify your missteps. You then have the golden opportunity to highlight the corrective actions that you instituted to right the wrongs. Chronicling your slip-ups on paper also permits you to express the lessons you've learned in their wake. Essentially, the mistake log functions as a constructive cleanup after the mistake train rolls through. Television writer and producer Gary Marshall wrote in his memoirs, "It's always helpful to learn from your mistakes because then your mistakes seem worthwhile."

11. Know Your Business

If you need information on a particular company to supplement your job search, or for any other reason, you would be well served by stopping by BusinessWire.com. This website is replete with up-to-the-minute corporate press releases, regulatory filings, and so on. In other words, business stuff that is hot off the press.

12. Sometimes Take the Roads Most Traveled

Metaphorically speaking, it's generally a prudent idea to take the roads least traveled. It's critical that we blaze our own trails in life, chart our own destinies. And, of course, there's less traffic on these roads. Nevertheless, in the smart game, it's always sensible to know what your fellow world travelers are doing, talking about, and uncovering in their adventures. The reality is that there are always a few diamonds in the rough and tumble of what's popular.

So, peruse the bestseller book lists. Take note of television show ratings and what's hot. Learn what products and services are popular with the masses, and what people are saying about them. This list could go on and on.

You might want to check out Web100.com, which lists the most popular websites in a broad range of categories. Being ignorant of all that's transpiring around you is not going to help you get the job you hunger for. It's not going to make you a more social animal, either. And it's certainly not going to make you smarter.

13. Know Your Rights

We live in a nation of laws. We also reside in a country that affords its citizenry certain inalienable rights. So, it behooves you to know exactly what these rights are in concert with the muddle of laws and regulations that exist on the multiple levels of government—federal, state, and local.

There are, in fact, innumerable instances in life when we could use a little—and sometimes more than a little—legal advice. The trouble is that most lawyers charge a pretty penny to dispense said advice. Fortunately, there's the information superhighway. Before making a decision as to whether or not we need to hire the genuine—and expensive—article, we can access in the virtual ether healthy doses of free counsel in areas ranging from employment rights to wills to landlords to pets. Worth checking out in this regard is Nolo Press at NoloPress.com, which bills itself as "Everyday Law for Everyday People."

14. Take an IQ Test

Taking an IQ test will measure your mental capacity vis-à-vis people your own age, not make you smarter per se. However, the mere act of taking an IQ test is wont to stir your brain and put you in the crosshairs of the thinking gun, just like the good old days when you were in school. And, in the process, you might just discover how smart you really are. There are multiple online IQ tests that you can take free of charge at various websites, including IQTest.com and IntelligentTest.com. The latter also features assorted mind games, puzzles, and brainteasers.

15. Lift Some Weights

You may associate weight lifting with muscleheads who don't have much going on in their upstairs apartments. Perish the thought! Lifting weights is renowned for increasing bone density, enhancing circulation, and—here's the real kicker—releasing the chemicals of the brain known as endorphins. Yes, a little weight lifting added to that get-smart stew of yours could certainly add flavor to the final product.

16. Play Smart

There are all kinds of games you can play with your friends. Likewise, there are multiple games you can play when you are all alone. Why not opt for the ones that will make you smarter, or at least exercise your brain as much as possible? Combine leisure and relaxation with healthy doses of thinking and brain stimulation. Play games like Scrabble and chess with others. Pull out the Rubik's cube when you're all by your lonesome.

17. Rely on Memory When Possible

In this day and age, we have so many devices to assist us in remembering things. The downside is that these very advances in technology often supplant old-fashioned memory power. We don't have to remember phone numbers anymore, because they're stored in our phones. We don't have to remember e-mails, because they're stored in our address books. It's no stretch to say that people used to memorize a lot more things back in the day. And, over the long haul, this is a good thing.

As it relates to the topic at hand, *Are You Smarter Than a 5th Grader?* is a most revealing show. It seems that kids in grade school are compelled to memorize a mother lode of things as part of their various lesson plans. It's what we all experienced. As time wore on, however, we let slip from our memory banks so much of what we had learned.

So, yes, the fifth graders rule in this arena. Very few us remember how to do algebra problems anymore. We don't recall the exact years of the California Gold Rush, either. How many elements on the periodic table could we name? Why not try to awaken the fifth grader within you by committing your grocery shopping lists to memory from now on. Then try your hand—or brain, as it were—in memorizing phone numbers and e-mails without any assists from machines.

18. Put the Calculator On Ice

A giant leap in the smart game could be accomplished by merely downgrading the role of your calculator. Add and subtract figures on a piece of paper or, better yet, in your head—*on your own*. This basic math is a simple but very effective way to stimulate your brain and make it more resilient and at the ready to handle other challenges that come your way.

19. Work at Different Jobs

If you're working part-time to plug the income gap until you find a permanent position, it certainly helps to experience new job challenges. Do things you've never done before. In the end, you'll be smarter for it. For instance, working in a restaurant kitchen could teach you an awful lot, including some useful new skills. It may, in fact, teach you that you never want to go near one again. Nevertheless, the larger point here is that working in different kinds of jobs with different kinds of people adds layers to your character and overall know-how.

20. Try New Things All Across the Board

Just as working different jobs can enlarge your smarts, the same logical reasoning applies to just about everything else that is new to you. In other words, work at tasks at which you're not especially proficient. After all, doing the same things that you are adept at time and again doesn't teach you anything new. But toiling in areas with which you are totally unfamiliar, or not especially adroit, has the potential to fortify your life résumé.

What kinds of things are we talking about? Instead of hiring a housepainter, paint a room for yourself. Instead of calling in a geeky neighbor to install a new computer system for you, try following the instructions without a helping hand. And this *new* stuff applies all across the board. That is, sample new foods at restaurants and while cooking in your home. Travel to places you've never before seen. Patronize unusual shops. Volunteer places and join clubs.

PART THREE

KICKING BACK

Twenty Ways to Reduce Stress

In times of stress, be bold and valiant.

—Horace, ancient Roman poet

Stress is often referred to as a silent killer. It is linked to multiple diseases and assorted afflictions. Granted, it cannot always be identified as the root cause of this illness or that sickness, but there's little doubt in medical circles that undue stress exacerbates and indeed instigates countless serious maladies from headaches to high blood pressure to heart disease. It is often a precursor to bouts of insomnia, depression, and impaired concentration.

The bottom line is that extreme emotional stress is bad for mind, body, and soul. It is bad for the short term and bad in the long term. The anxiety that constitutes stress is worth waging war against at every turn. Most especially in your unemployed state of being, it behooves you to be ever vigilant in deflecting the slings and arrows that stress throws your way. You might want to visit the American Institute of Stress at Stress.org. This nonprofit institute is chock full of information on the subject matter, including the myriad symptoms of stress and ways to combat it.

Here's some assorted food for thought on potential stress busters:

1. Eat a Balanced Diet

A healthy, well balanced diet goes a long way toward minimizing stress. For starters, scale back on your intake of sugars and salts. Go green with lots of green vegetables and green tea, for instance, in lieu of excessive caffeine.

2. Clean Up Your Living Space

Residing in an orderly, clean environment is better for both your physical *and* emotional health. So, make your bed every day, frequently vacuum the rugs, and dust the furniture. Don't leave the dirty dishes in the sink overnight, and take out the garbage before the fruit flies discover your discarded banana peels and watermelon rinds. By osmosis, you get a lift—even if it's a minimal one—from residing in spick and span living quarters. There's not a single good reason for you to call a bona fide pigsty home.

3. Drink in Moderation

If you like to sample the grape, or the hops, barley, and corn in their spirited incarnations, keep the imbibing to a minimum. Excessive alcohol consumption during stressful times in your life may supply you with momentary illusions of relaxation, but—rest assured—these hazy mirages will quickly evaporate. And in their wake will be the multiple markings of stress—both physical and emotional—more unsightly and injurious than ever before.

4. Employ Time Management

Adding to the obvious benefits of residing in a clean and well-ordered setting, there are comparable benefits in more or less scheduling your day. Plan to do certain things at certain times—and do them! Get out and about as often as you possibly can. Don't squander precious hours—even though you've got more of them to play with these days—by sitting around and stewing in your juices. Stewing juices make for a very bitter brew and, in fact, are loaded with the ingredients of stress.

5. Have More Than a Few Laughs

Granted, things may not seem all that funny when you're not cashing weekly paychecks and whistling in the wind on the way to the bank. Nevertheless, now more than ever is the time for you to have a few laughs in as many venues as possible. Socialize with family and friends (at least the funny ones). Rent comedic movies. Read funny books. Inspect humorous websites, such as ComedyCentral.com, StupidVideos.com, and Fark.com.

6. Take Long Walks

Ah, yes, this same advice rears its head once more. Get out in the fresh air and take frequent and lengthy walks. This simple act is a notorious stress reliever. Of course, it's important that you let your feet do their walking in non-stressful surroundings. In other words, don't walk alongside belching smokestacks, busy traffic, or sidewalks crammed with souls who would more than likely contribute to the elevation of your stress level. And you know who these people are.

Unemployment Benefit #23

Your nose is no longer subject to the wafting aromas of people pickled in perfume or cologne.

7. Repair What Needs Repairing

Don't allow things to fall into disrepair. In more anecdotal language, if a door falls off its hinges, don't go on living without the door. Put it back up! Don't be left in the dark because a light bulb burns out—replace it! Tighten loose screws wherever they happen to lose their grip. If your window blinds fall down, put them back up instead of covering the window with a bed sheet. When all is said and done, you feel better when things are running like a well-oiled machine. In fact, when everything is working, it makes you more apt to believe that you'll be working in the very near future, too.

8. Plant a Garden

Planting a garden is a helpful stress reducer. If you don't have a plot of soil to till in the great outdoors, caring for a few houseplants in your apartment will suffice. It's just that living things add life, so to speak, to otherwise lifeless surroundings.

Outdoor gardens and indoor plants alike require meticulous attention. And the beauty of both outdoor gardening and tending to indoor plants is that your choices are more plentiful than ever before. Even if you live in a skyscraper in a big city, you are not limited to decorative plants. There are many small trees, herbs, and vegetables that grow very nicely indoors. Tomato plants that produce ample fruits from pots inside the house are now readily available. For a wheelbarrow full of information on this popular subject matter, drop by HouseplantGrowing.com and GardenersNet.com.

9. Practice Autogenics

If you're unfamiliar with autogenics, it is, in a nutshell, a practice that asks you to wade through a series of visualizations to engender a state of meditative relaxation. Fathered by German psychiatrist Johannes Schultz in 1932, this yoga-like deliberation is designed to, foremost, assuage stress-induced emotional turmoil—to turn the ubiquitous fight-or-flight response on its proverbial head.

Among many things, autogenics can lend a hand in reducing tension, lowering your blood pressure, and taming irritable bowel syndrome. For additional information on autogenics training, comb these websites on the matter before us: Stress.About.com and Higher-Self-Improvement-Pursuits.com.

10. Utilize Aromatherapy

There is something warm and reassuring about certain wafting aromas that have an uncanny knack for turning stress on its head. If the odor in question is three-day-old garbage rapidly decaying in ninety-five degree heat and brutal humidity, that's not going to do the trick. If, however, it's particular plant oils, including essential oils, you've got the ticket for an emotional and physical boost. Visit AromaWeb.com for more information on this sweet-smelling New Age stress buster.

11. Don't Procrastinate

Do what you have to do today. Do what you said you were going to do today—today! Procrastination amounts to a stress-building snowball.

Napoleon Hill once said, "Procrastination is the bad habit of putting off until the day after tomorrow what should have been done the day before yesterday."

Procrastination is not something you want to let bowl you over. It all comes back to being active and proactive during your unemployment days and nights. If you are always *doing*—and, especially, doing what you have to do—you'll feel better about yourself. If you don't do what you know you should be doing, you'll assume armfuls of stress that you otherwise wouldn't have to bear.

12. Avoid Doomsayers

The last thing you need in your life now are people who see the glass as half empty—or, more likely, completely empty. Let's face it: There are certain persons in our lives who are the embodiment of negative energy morning, noon, and night. These are the very folks you should avoid like the plague at this time in your life.

Regrettably, there are boatloads of men and women who have nothing good to say about anything, and who see only doom and gloom on the horizon—both yours and theirs. For most of these people, a person without a paying job is a ticking time bomb waiting to explode in their frightened faces. They view joblessness as akin to some kind of leprosy. And, worst of all, they see you as a pathetic loser unworthy of their empathy. But the reality is that they cannot empathize with you, because they don't have it in them. So, all you can do is avoid these creatures of the night as much as humanly possible—even if they happen to be your kith and kin.

Unemployment Benefit #24

You are no longer the protagonist of some of the juiciest gossip in the workplace.

13. Employ Anger Management

Try to keep your anger and rage to a bare minimum. In other words, don't sweat the small things and blow your top at the drop of a hat. If, for instance, a mother with an extremely bratty kid is seated beside you in the unemployment office, take a deep breath and move away if possible. If somebody cuts you off on the highway, don't spit fire—forget about it and arrive at your intended destination in one piece and as relaxed as possible.

Remember what Ralph Kramden's doctor prescribed for stress in a classic *Honeymooners* episode? He told the irascible Ralph to recite this little ditty anytime he felt the seeds of anger sprouting up inside of him: "Pins and needles. Needles and pins. A happy man is a man that grins." After audibly vocalizing this simple verse, Ralph was importuned to pose a question to himself: "What am I mad about?" And, lo and behold, he couldn't remember. Well, in Ralph's particular case, this therapy tamed the anger beast for a nanosecond. Nevertheless, the larger point here is that you should save your angry outbursts—and your internal seething—for the genuine articles and not the piddling encounters of daily living. You'll keep a lot of stress at arm's length by charting this course.

14. View Your Problems as Challenges

This may, in fact, sound a little corny and something more suited for a Tony Robbins CD. But, the truth be told, it's something you absolutely need to do in order to confront stress head on and defeat it. Problems such as unemployment can be quite daunting—almost debilitating in their width and breadth—but, alas, this is part of life.

If you look at joblessness as a major challenge rather than a monstrous obstacle in life's path, all things will unfold more smoothly, particularly on the emotional side of the ledger. Many of the greatest success stories in life revolve around individuals who were down and out for a spell. But each one of them grabbed hold of life's reins and turned chicken feathers into chicken cordon bleu.

15. Get a Good Night's Sleep

When your body is sleep deprived, your mind is similarly on the prowl for forty winks. Lack of sleep compounds stress. So, while you are alive, alert, awake, and aware, call on SleepFoundation.org. This organization will furnish you with a mother lode of tips on getting a quality night's sleep, such as avoiding strenuous exercise in the evening. Other sage counsel: Steer clear of alcohol and caffeine by night.

16. Take a Hot Bath or Shower

Under certain circumstances, it's a good thing to do in the middle of the day. Take a soothing hot bath or shower (and a refreshing cool one in the heat of the summer). There is something to be said for getting revitalized when you need it most—and that could be at three o'clock in the afternoon after a wearisome job search. Of course, for a good night's sleep, a nice hot bath before bedtime is known to work wonders, too.

17. Try a Little Music Therapy

Oliver Wendell Holmes wrote: "Take a music bath once or twice a week for a few seasons. You will find it is to the soul what a water bath is to the body." Indeed, music therapy of some note is an often-employed stress reliever with a longstanding tradition. This brand of therapy spans a lot of musical scales, if you will, from listening to your relaxing favorites to devising song lyrics to literally performing somewhere. The latter could be in a church choir; it could be in a karaoke bar. It doesn't much matter where as long as—in the end—it reduces your stress level. Reflect on what Cervantes said a long time ago: "He who sings scares away his woes."

Unemployment Benefit #25

As never before, you can get in touch with your inner Rip Van Winkle.

18. Get Hold of an Anti-Stress Prop

Believe it or not, there's actually a cottage industry devoted to stress toys and stress balls. Most of these pieces of merchandise are manufactured with squeezeability foremost in mind. You get to exercise your hands and relieve stress by squeezing and pulling at products manufactured in every conceivable incarnation.

Take out your frustrations and release your tension buildup by crushing a banker pig toy or widescreen TV toy. Grab hold of an eyeball or golf-ball stress ball and apply all the pressure you can muster. Release as much stress as is physically possible through these little exercises. If you are interested in feasting your eyes on the "World's Largest Stress Ball Selection," Bluetrack.com (1-800-790-6090) is where you ought to head.

19. Communicate with the Fellow Stressed-Out

You are not alone—not by any stretch of the imagination! So, locate people to talk with about your anxieties and the various stresses in your life brought on by unemployment. Look to the Internet, too, for discussion groups on this very important and quite universal subject matter. Visit Forums.About.com and search for the stress management discussion. Pose questions and receive advice in return. Weigh in with your thoughts. Tell the world what works for you as a stress buster and, of course, what causes you the most stress in your life.

20. Travel the World at Your Computer

If you haven't yet gone on this global adventure, it's highly recommended as a stress reliever, in addition to being quite fascinating. Visit Google Earth at Earth.Google.com and download the free software on-site. This simple act gets you packed and ready to travel the world in a matter of minutes. And the beauty of this brand of jet setting is that there are no airline security concerns here for you to wade through. If getting on an airplane nowadays isn't a stress producer, then nothing is.

Yes, sitting at your computer in the comforts of home sweet home, you can type in physical street addresses from around the globe and fast find yourself with bird's eye aerial views of the chosen areas. You can venture to landmarks near and far. Have you lived in a former neighborhood that you'd like to revisit? Type in your old address and off you go. Vacationed somewhere a while back? Go back again, but this time on the cheap. Fly halfway around the world in a matter of seconds. See the sights of Europe and Asia from on high, as it were, and never have to fret over the currency exchange rate or the weak dollar.

CHAPTER FOURTEEN

Twenty Relaxation Possibilities

Sometimes the cure for restlessness is rest.

—Colleen Wainwright

To add a little whipped cream to the chocolate pudding that was our prior discussion on waging war against stress, the roster to come is a smorgasbord of additional relaxation tips, tools, and techniques. Consider this assortment of ideas the verbal equivalent of a Whitman's Sampler. The eclectic suggestions selected can aid and abet you in reducing your stress levels—for sure—but also empower you, in many instances, to have a grand old time. A few of the possibilities that follow are intended to put you on the road of quiet contemplation. There's definitely something for everyone here—a veritable vegetable soup for the unemployed person's soul.

1. Close Your Eyes and Recall a Happy Time

Pull your time machine out of the closet, polish it up a bit, and return to yesteryear, even if yesteryear is yesterday. Just sit back and relax while recalling an idyllic event in your life, or perhaps a single moment or extra-special day. Elvis Presley made famous the sentiment, "Memories sweeten through the ages just like wine." Take heed of the King of Rock-and-Roll's warm and reassuring words and hark back to happy times, happy places, and happy people. It's a surefire way to relax your body and soothe your soul.

Unemployment Benefit #26

You are free from any and all co-workers talking on speakerphone with their office door wide open.

2. Recall a Funny Memory

"The more you find out about the world, the more opportunities there are to laugh at it," said Bill Nye. So, while still in our recollecting mode, there are other regions of your past that are worth mining. Summon up the lighter moments and the amusing anecdotes that you've amassed through the years. Conjure up specific events and certain persons from days gone by—memories of people, places, and times that evoke everything from simple smiles to roll-on-the-floor fits of laughter.

To illustrate the larger point about how recalling an amusing moment or funny person can turn tears to laughter, let's turn back the clock to August 1974. There we find the president of the United States only minutes away from delivering his resignation speech to a national audience. To make a very long story short, this snapshot in time was—quite understandably—an emotional whirlwind for the man exiting the highest office in the land, as well as for the country at large.

Ensnared in the Watergate political scandal, President Richard Nixon was more than a little weepy-eyed as the television network cameras and their hot lights readied for action. And since a touch of makeup was the order of the day before anybody who was anybody faced the aforementioned cameras, a dilemma of epic proportions loomed large. Most fortunately, veteran CBS makeup artist Lillian Brown was on the scene to effectively turn tears to laughter and keep the historical ball rolling forward. As a matter of record, she recounted this story to veteran newsman Roger Mudd for his recent book, *The Place to Be*, more than a quarter of a century after it happened.

You see, several years prior, Ms. Brown had shared a bizarre experience with the president. By chance at a White House Christmas party, the twosome corralled his overly rambunctious Irish setter and proceeded to lock the dog in a bathroom, hoping to keep the antsy canine there until the evening's festivities were over. But the *pièce de résistance* to this remembrance is that while CBS makeup artist Lillian Brown and President of the United States Richard Nixon were wholly successful in locking in the playful pooch, they unwittingly locked themselves in the very same bathroom.

The recounting of this amusing anecdote—just moments before the President's scheduled address—instantaneously stopped Mr. Nixon's waterfall of tears and brought a big smile to his face. And, as they say, the rest is history. The President had his makeup applied, delivered his speech on time, and left office the following day. Who knows what may have happened had Lillian Brown not been there with such a quirky personal memory at her ready disposal to lift a depressed man's spirits?

And the beauty is that you don't need anybody to assist you in recalling the good times and humorous happenings in your life. You could do it yourself while sitting in your easy chair, lying in bed, or dining at the kitchen table. All you need are the memories—and you've no doubt got a wealth of them.

3. Look at Old Pictures

There's nothing quite like strolling down memory lane for a well-deserved bit of rest and relaxation. And since it's been said, "One picture is worth a thousand words," why don't you pull out the photo albums or the box full of pictures in your closet? Turn on your favorite music and plow through them. For added pleasure and repose, write commentary on the reverse sides of each photo. Just a sentence or two will do.

4. Have a Communication-free Day

Since so much of contemporary living revolves around sitting in front of a computer screen, blabbing on cell phones with mercurial reception, sending inane text messages, and watching hundreds of cable television channels, why not institute—for twenty-four hours—a communication-free day? It'll certainly be something unusual—a trailblazing day in your life that may lead you to places you never dream existed.

So, don't log onto the Internet, don't check your e-mail, don't text message, don't answer your cell phone, don't watch your TV, and, for good measure, don't read the day's newspapers. Stay in the complete dark for a day. Ironically, being in the dark for a bit can sometimes show you the light. In fact, this brief timeout from twenty-first-century ways could just clear your mind and make you more lucid in the ensuing days of your job search.

5. Read a Book in the Great Outdoors

For most of us, reading is strictly an indoor experience. But if you haven't taken a book into the natural light of day, you don't know what you're missing. So, what are you waiting for? Grab a book and head to the nearest park or sandy beach. Read under the sun. It's one of the most inexpensive tickets to relaxation, particularly if you borrow the book from the library.

Unemployment Benefit #27

You can get up bright and early to watch the sunrise ... and then go back to bed.

6. Visit a Body of Water

By our very nature, we the people are drawn to water. And, no, this particular entry has gotten nothing to do with showering and bathing in the tub, which, albeit watery experiences, are different kettles of fish altogether. Rather, it's about the bodies of water in the palm of Mother Nature's hand—everything from magnificent oceans to meandering rivers to serene lakes to babbling brooks.

Pretty much wherever there is a picturesque geographic locale with water in the backdrop, you will find people, and sometimes a whole lot of people. As a relaxing jaunt, there's perhaps no better advice than to head to water. It could be a nearby beach, a riverbank, a pond full of goldfish, or even a sluggish stream in a neighboring park. Whether it's a waterhole or a waterfall, it's apt to advance introspective moments of relaxation.

7. Visit an Old Graveyard

This may sound like a somewhat ghoulish suggestion, but it's anything but. Old graveyards, cemeteries, burial grounds—whatever they are called—are everywhere. Sometimes they're associated with churches. Sometimes they stand alone as historical markers of what once was. But what each one of them has in common is old headstones or grave markers of some sort denoting the final resting spots of people who previously walked the earth.

Visiting these consecrated grounds is a remarkable adventure on several levels. Foremost, the vast majority of these burial spots are situated in tranquil environs—although many can be found in the heart of big cities. (For instance, Trinity Church and graveyard—where the guy on the ten-dollar-bill, Alexander Hamilton, is buried—is located in lower Manhattan on the periphery of Ground Zero.) But even in crowded metropolitan centers, these places are invariably peaceful locales. In addition to the very welcome quietude, the headstones therein often sport names that are now quite curious to our ears. The various grave markers frequently boast intriguing verse and sometimes very moving poetry, too. And, yes, there are plenty of gravestones that bear the immortal words, "Here lies … "

While paying your respects at old graveyards, you also have the rare opportunity to reflect on the fact that your human ancestors trod the very same soil as you, even if so much of it is now covered in concrete. At these final resting places, you are in the company of reposing souls—men and women who exited this mortal coil hundreds of years ago. For sure, it was a different world and different planet back then. You can appreciate how a stopover at a burial site from the past is potentially a very relaxing side trip. It's fraught with countless openings to reflect on the meaning of life.

8. Watch Fun and Ridiculous Videos on YouTube

So much of contemporary living is a spirited tug-of-war between Internet adventures and old-fashioned shoe leather escapades. This entire book bears this out with its ping-pong fusion of suggestions for maximizing what both virtual reality and the great outdoors have to offer.

So, back to cyberspace we go for a relaxing stream of diversionary fluff. For some easy relaxation, visit YouTube.com and comb the site for fun and ridiculous videos to at once entertain you and lower your blood pressure. YouTube has it all, including clips from television shows and movies—and sometimes the whole enchilada! It has every imaginable original production from the regular folks. Foul-ups and blunders by public figures and non-public figures alike, which are captured for posterity on camera, are almost certain to land on YouTube. In fact, the site has afforded scores of people their fifteen minutes of fame, including some individuals who would rather not have had it, such as Miss Teen South Carolina. In any event, YouTube's got a treasure trove of entertainment for you with perpetual new stuff barreling down the pike. Search for videos in such categories as Entertainment, Comedy, Pets & Animals, People & Blogs, and Sports—and, by all means, relax.

9. Sip a Relaxing Beverage

Just as what you eat is important to your overall health and wellness, so too is what you drink. If relaxation is your immediate goal, there are certain beverages known to aid you in getting to that serene state of mind and body, including green tea, hot chocolate, hot milk, and—yes—red and white wines (in moderation, of course).

10. Maintain a Good Posture

You know the modeling cliché of comely women walking to and fro with hardcover books delicately balanced atop their pretty heads? Well, it is all about good posture. And strange as this might seem, the proper posture is a precursor to a relaxed body. And a relaxed body is the precursor to relaxed mind. A relaxed mind, in turn, will help you find the job or career that you truly desire. So, stand up straight. Don't slump in your chair. Walk with your head up and shoulders back.

Don't believe good posture is that important? Chew on a few of the deleterious consequences of poor posture: neck strain, lower back pain, and carpal tunnel syndrome. A good posture is renowned for making you appear taller, slimmer, and both more at ease and confident. And when you look more at ease and confident, you usually are. So, get with the posture program.

11. Ride a Bicycle

Not only is bicycle riding a relaxing pastime. It's also good exercise. And, if you get sufficiently acclimated to the bicycle, it can replace the automobile in many instances as your choice of transportation. This can save you a few dollars in your travels and reduce your contribution to ozone layer depletion.

12. Cavort with Your Best Friend on Four Legs

If you have a companion animal—that's what household pets are called these days—you've got a bona fide friend. Pets are renowned for engendering relaxation. Pet therapy, for instance, is an increasingly popular practice in which cats, dogs, small animals, and domesticated birds are brought into locales where people can use a pick-me-up of some kind. Nursing homes, hospices, and special education schools are just a few of the places where these animals make appearances to spread a little cheer where cheer is in short supply.

The most popular pets—cats and dogs—comprise a considerable demographic of innocent, nonjudgmental personalities, which are just what the doctored ordered vis-à-vis easy moments and good times. After all, your cat or dog is not going to think any less of you when you're out of work. Neither feline nor canine will hound you about the seriousness or lack thereof of your daily job hunt, and whether you're doing enough to find employment. In other words, listen to your cat purr. Appreciate your dog's contented pant after a Frisbee frolic in the park.

If you have neither pooch nor pussycat, try visiting an animal shelter—you just may come home with a new friend.

13. Turn Your Mattress Over Frequently

Do you realize that if you turn your mattress over every few days, it'll supply you with a better night's sleep? It's true. Unless your mattress is ready to be put out with the trash, turning it over is the closest thing there is to getting new one. So, as long as the springs aren't protruding out of it and into your back, give it flip every few days—or once a week—and you'll reap the sleep benefits without expending a plug nickel.

14. Sleep with the Fish

You can achieve an ocean full of serenity by merely staring into a tank full of colorful tropical fish—without a seeming care in the world— rhythmically completing their laps. Indeed, to watch fish contentedly swimming to and fro is undeniably a tranquil pause from life's daily grind. For this reason alone, many people are calling the aquarium hobby their own.

If you don't have an aquarium on the premises—and can't afford to start one at this uncertain time in your life—you might want to go someplace where there is one. Try a friend's or relative's house; a business lobby with an attractive setup; a retailer who sells aquarium trappings; or, better yet, an aquarium, open to the general public, with fish more commonly found in the high seas. Granted, the latter may not always supply relaxation. Gazing into a shark tank can be a wee bit unsettling. But, generally speaking, peering into a tank full of fish is enough to make you want to join them—à la *The Incredible Mr. Limpet*—in their watery Shangri-La. And, if interacting with the genuine article is problematic, you could always employ an aquarium screen saver, which is the next best thing to the real thing.

Unemployment Benefit #28

Whatever it happens to be, you have the time to begin— and maybe even complete—your magnum opus.

15. Watch a Classic Television Show

Nowadays, the reality show is all the rage. And they most definitely have their place as entertainment. But there comes a time—for relaxation purposes—when we'd rather not watch a family intervention to save a drug-addled relation; or a wife confronting her serial adulterer husband; or a washed up and whiny celebrity bemoaning the fact that he can't get work. These are the moments to tune in to *Leave It to Beaver*, *I Love Lucy*, or whatever television shows from the past best quench your thirst for nostalgia.

It doesn't matter that the Cleavers were not actually representative of the average American family of the late 1950s and early 1960s. It doesn't matter that the Wild West wasn't as clean and pressed as Marshall Matt Dillon's shirt and slacks, which were more often than not pristine, even after a lengthy shoot-'em-up chase through a scorching hot and very dusty desert. It doesn't matter that *Perry Mason* justice wasn't quite the same as American justice. It was all good entertainment from a simpler time—when blackberries were only found on bushes and in fruit stores and supermarkets—and that's why so many of us can't get enough of them now.

16. Conduct Your Favorite Music

Consider this something of an addendum to our previous discussion on music therapy. It's sure to give you a lift. Put on your favorite CD, or get cranking a preferred selection in your iPod or MP3 player, and start conducting to the rhythm of the music. Imagine you're Keith Lockhart in front of the Boston Pops Orchestra. Grab any available baton-like instrument in your home—a feather duster or kitchen spatula will suffice—and conduct until you drop.

17. Mine Your Hobby

If you've got a hobby, mine it now for all it's worth in the rest and relaxation department. If, for instance, your hobby finds you a collector of anything from stamps to bling to Beanie Babies, go through the entire collection with the proverbial fine-toothed comb. You could meticulously inventory your collection from soup to nuts, describing the condition and market value of each piece within it. There's no reason why you can't get hours of uninterrupted pleasure out of your particular hobby. That's what hobbies are for, aren't they?

18. Revisit a Place Full of Happy Memories

While running to and fro in the work safari, why not budget a little time to return to a physical location infused with fond memories? Maybe you haven't been back to your old alma mater in quite some time—graduation day, perhaps? Well, if practical, revisit the campus. Return to your high school or grade school. Is there an old neighborhood of yours that you'd like to see again? Go there! The sky's the limit in this arena, because we've all been places and lived in places with, hopefully, more than a few happy experiences along the way.

Unemployment Benefit #29

You can shower at one o'clock in the afternoon and remain under the pulsating jets of water for as long as your heart desires … or as long as there is sufficient hot water.

19. Get a Massage

If you need to physically draw relaxation from your weary and worried body, consider patronizing a masseuse. Try IWantAMassage.com to help you locate one nearby. Or, if you're not in a position to plunk down the requisite dollars for the service, find someone who can give you an amateur massage, which is certainly better than nothing at all. In fact, it can be a whole lot better than the professional job, depending, of course, on who's the masseuse.

20. Create a Work of Art

Awaken the artist within you right now! If you've sat in front of a canvas before with brush and palette in hand, it's time to kick it up a notch and paint your Rembrandt. If you've dabbled in crafts, do more than dabble and create something worthy of selling in stores or on eBay. If you've got writing aptitude, formulate a book idea. Nonfiction book notions are, more often than not, sold with book proposals. That is, you don't need to complete an entire book beforehand, just a comprehensive outline and sample materials. For you aspiring novel writers out there—sorry. You've got to have the whole deal done before pitching it, unless, of course, you're Mary Higgins Clark, Nicholas Sparks, or some other proven quantity.

If you desire information on the elements of a book proposal, there are several literary agent websites that supply you with samples. Among the resources at SmallPress.org is a lucid description of proposal writing. If you've got the finished product on hand—nonfiction proposal or completed novel manuscript—you might want to query a literary agent and try to obtain representation to the book trade. Most large and mid-size publishing houses will only look at materials represented by an agent. One helpful site in locating potential agents, with descriptions of what they represent and how to approach them, is the Association of Authors' Representatives at AAR-Online.org, which lists its active membership. Publishers Marketplace at PublishersMarketplace.com is an interesting place for aspiring authors to peruse and has literary agents as members. A more general site for writers is Writers Net at WritersNet.com, which is replete with information and discussions on the publishing process, including the role of literary agents.

ƒ Primer on Meditation

Some people think that meditation takes time away from physical accomplishment.

Taken to extremes, of course, that's true.

Most people, however, find that meditation creates more time than it takes.

—Peter McWilliams

There are infinite forms of meditation and meditative passageways. In fact, we've already touched upon a couple of disciplines that incorporate meditation principles into their practices—yoga and autogenics, for example. But right now we're going to supply you with a decidedly simple—but remarkably practical— meditative regimen that you can effortlessly implement in all kinds of settings and at all times during the day.

Regular stretching movements are common sense. They are hardly unique to calisthenics classes or the aforementioned practices. With the assistance of martial-arts sensei and fifth-degree blackbelt Thomas Nigro, who taught karate and meditation methods to students of all ages both here and abroad, you are about to receive a series of user-friendly stretching exercises. Each one has been carefully selected with you in mind. They are recommended exercises for the unemployed minions who are, quite understandably, under a mother lode of stress. They are also recommended when you're duly employed and likewise cannibalized by the stress monster.

Our bodies are crying out to be loosened and stretched. When they become accustomed to getting a routine workout, they welcome more challenging movements, including advanced exercises. Without proper stretching exercises, physically involved sports, for example, are awkward at best and injurious at worst. So, mastering the basics is job one—beginning at the beginning, if you will.

The basic techniques of the various exercises to follow are applicable along all of life's highways and byways. In other words, these stretching exercises are for your daily fare, not only today, but tomorrow, and next year, too. They include:

+ Head rolls
+ Triangulars
+ Heel/toe bends

Why not take ten to fifteen minutes to stretch your body at the beginning of each day? Or, perhaps, before you embark on your job hunt? When you come home physically and emotionally exhausted after a grueling job interview is a prime time to do some stretching. Stretch your body; stretch your mind. Let's get stretching.

Head Rolls

A head roll is the simplest of all stretching exercises. If you have a head and a neck, you're a good candidate for this straightforward and effective workout. And the beauty of it is that it can be practiced in your living room, at your computer desk, outside in the wide-open spaces—anywhere at all for that matter. So, let's roll:

1. With your chin closely aligned to your chest—but not quite touching it—gently roll your head in a counterclockwise direction, completing a full circle.
2. After several counterclockwise revolutions of your head, switch to a clockwise direction and repeat the process.
3. Repeat this routine for as long as you feel comfortable. Do not permit yourself to become dizzy.

Triangulars

Triangulars are also practical exercises to incorporate into your daily routine. Like head rolls, employ them before you begin your daily job search, after you come home from a full day of activity, before cooking your supper, and so on. In fact, any time that fits your schedule is a good time to do these movements. Here's what you need to know:

1. Spread your legs as far apart as you can, while making certain to remain comfortable.
2. Stand erect and stretch your left hand to the sky, palm facing inward and fingers pointing straight up. Keep your feet firmly planted on the floor.
3. Turn your right hip slightly inward to the front and lean your right shoulder over your turned inward hip, leaving your right hand hanging towards the floor. You should feel your hip turning into your rib cage.

4. For maximum stretching while in this position, reach for the sky with your left hand and the floor with your right hand.

5. Remain in this position for one to two minutes before reversing sides.

Heel/Toe Bends

This is still another very accessible exercise that you'd be wise to include in your regular exercise routine. To perform heel/toe bends:

1. Stand your feet shoulder-distance apart.
2. With your palms facing each other and fingers pointing upwards, stretch both of your fully extended arms over your head.
3. While reaching skyward with both arms, rise up on your toes.
4. Lower your arms as you return to your flat feet, and then proceed to touch your toes.
5. Repeat this procedure at a rapid pace.
   Simple stretching is focused on the key parts of the body:
   + The neck with the head rolls.
   + The back with the triangulars and heel/toe bends.
   + The legs with the heel/toe bends.

Stretch not only for daily exercise. Use these specific stretches for relaxation purposes and stress reduction. Make certain to always incorporate proper breathing into all of your stretching exercises. Never hold your breath. You should be breathing at a relaxed pace into the nose and out through the mouth. In and of themselves, simple deep breathing exercises are an effective means of stretching. Yes—stretching. You can perform such breathing exercises anywhere and at any time!

Remember, when your stretching regimen is complete, your body should feel:

+ Resilient
+ Relaxed
+ Energized

So, if you reach a point in your unemployment adventures and misadventures when the weight of the world is on your shoulders, take a few moments for yourself. Mentally remove yourself from the job safari. Stretch a bit. Transfer your thoughts away from your former boss, your pile of bills, and résumé writing. And when you return to your actual life in progress, you'll very likely find yourself refreshed with a renewed energy to forge ahead with both calmness and confidence.

Twenty Films that Will Lift Your Spirits

Hollywood is where, if you don't have happiness, you send out for it.

—Rex Reed

Since you've got a little extra time these days and a simultaneous need to be inspired, you might want to pop in a DVD of a film or two that'll accomplish this noble mission. What follows is a potpourri of movies from both the recent and not-so-recent past. Each one is entertaining, interesting, and inspiring on some level. This list is intentionally diverse, which guarantees that there is something for everyone.

Unemployment Benefit #30

You can go to a movie in the middle of the week in the middle of the day.

1. *The Pursuit of Happyness*

Will Smith
2006

Yes, that's the incorrect spelling of the word *happiness* but the correct spelling of the movie title. Watch the picture and you'll appreciate why. Regardless of the spelling of a word, this is a film that is truly an uplifting beacon for the unemployed minions. Based on a true story, *The Pursuit of Happyness* chronicles a segment of the life of salesman Christopher Gardner who—to make a rather long and complex story short and sweet—falls on very hard times and lands lock, stock, and barrel on the streets with a young son to care for. He weathers an ugly divorce, an IRS seizure of all his assets, homelessness, and jail time.

2. *We Are Marshall*

Matthew McConaughey
2006

When a plane carrying members of the Marshall University Thundering Herd football team, and some of its fans, crashed and killed all on board in 1970, a new coach and players were left to pick up the pieces and start anew. Based on this true story, *We Are Marshall* underscores the incredible resilience of human beings, even in their darkest hours.

3. *Field of Dreams*

Kevin Costner, Amy Madigan
1989

An Iowa farmer hears voices amidst his sprawling rows of cornstalks and concludes not that he is insane, but that he must build a baseball stadium amidst all of the future cornflakes and ethanol.

Among the ghostly utterances emanating from the green fields is one recurring sound bite: "If you build it ... they will come." If you go to FieldOfDreamsMovieSite.com, you may opt to rent this enduringly popular and uplifting movie.

4. *The Shawshank Redemption*

Tim Robbins, Morgan Freeman
1994

How does one achieve genuine redemption in this life? In this searing drama, two inmates at a maximum-security prison achieve their versions of it by helping one another and others rise above past injustices and the widespread brutality of life behind bars. While not a blockbuster hit upon its release, *The Shawshank Redemption* has nevertheless gained in popularity through the years, and is recognized as a remarkable movie with timeless messages of hope and deliverance. Visit ShawshankRedemption.org for more information on this stirring story.

5. *Lean on Me*

Morgan Freeman
1989

Based on a true story, this film recounts the transformation of a failing inner-city high school in the state of New Jersey. Desperately in need of a pick-me-up, a man named Joe Clark assumes the thankless duties of school principal. At once autocratic and completely dedicated to the job at hand, Clark's indefatigable tough love approach turns things around, proving that anything is possible.

6. *The Sound of Music*

Julie Andrews, Christopher Plummer
1965

This movie classic has it all: a love story, melodious musical numbers that just about everybody in the world is familiar with more than forty years later, and, alas, its fair share of creepy Nazis. *The Sound of Music* tells the story of the von Trapp family of Austria in the late 1930s, when the country was, for all intents and purposes, annexed by the German nation on the eve of a world war. For further information on the real von Trapp family—yes, they really existed—as well as the film classic, check out Sound-Of-Music.com.

7. *Mr. Holland's Opus*

Richard Dreyfuss
1995

This movie unfurls the story of a downcast and discontented music composer who, surprisingly, realizes genuine satisfaction as a high-school teacher. The film chronicles Mr. Holland's odyssey over a period of years and includes multiple side stories that'll surely tug at your heartstrings, as well as inspire you to place authentic satisfaction atop your job and career search agenda.

8. *Dead Poets Society*

Robin Williams
1989

John Keating turns his English class on to poetry and—what he perceives as—the true meaning of life. *Dead Poets Society* affords its audience an abundance of food for thought, quite a gut-punch plot twist, and a powerfully uplifting finale.

9. *On the Waterfront*

Marlon Brando, Karl Malden, Lee J. Cobb
1954

A washed-up prizefighter named Terry Malloy, played by Marlon Brando in his prime (before he became two Terry Malloys), finds himself toiling as a longshoreman on the rough and tumble docks dominated by mobsters. In the end, Malloy takes his licks, risks his own life and limbs, and stands up to the rampant corruption and the thugs who enforce it. *On the Waterfront* is quite justifiably regarded as one of the best films ever made—evocative in its gritty feel more than a half century later, and timeless in its abiding message of true courage winning the day in the face of seemingly insurmountable odds.

10. *Rocky*

Sylvester Stallone, Talia Shire
1976

When a two-bit boxer named Rocky Balboa gets a shot at the heavyweight championship of the world, you know you're in for some entertaining inspiration—and some sequels, too. *Yo, Adrian . . .*

11. *Rain Man*

Dustin Hoffman, Tom Cruise
1988

Avaricious yuppie Charlie Babbitt, learns that his recently deceased father's last will and testament left the preponderance of his significant fortune not to him, but to his autistic brother, Raymond. This scenario sets the stage for a very moving and—in the end—stirring cross-country journey shared by two brothers who couldn't be more different.

12. *The Color Purple*

Whoopi Goldberg, Danny Glover
1985

Based on the novel of the same name by Alice Walker, this movie—directed by Steven Spielberg—marks Whoopi Goldberg's big-screen debut and recounts the tale of young black girl suffering silently in a cruel, male-dominated environment. It's a story of tremendous valor and triumph against decidedly long odds.

13. *A River Runs Through It*

Craig Sheffer, Brad Pitt, Tom Skerritt
1992

Based on his own upbringing, this is novelist's Norman Maclean's tale of two brothers born to a Presbyterian minister and his wife in Missoula, Montana, during the first quarter of the twentieth century. Filmed on location in Big Sky Country, with an equally appealing musical score, this movie unfolds what is, yes, one family's tragedy, but also an inspiring life lesson for one and all. In addition, *A River Runs Through It* might make you want to take up fly fishing, too.

14. *Artificial Intelligence: AI*

Haley Joel Osment, Jude Law
2001

This admittedly unusual film is a futuristic story of an extraordinarily advanced boy robot by the name of David. Directed again by

Steven Spielberg, this movie's general theme is that love is genuine, even in a synthetic robot boy. Epic in its scope, look, and unshakable message, *AI* is considerably enhanced by a compelling musical score. After seeing this picture, you will want the CD of its soundtrack.

15. *Bad Day at Black Rock*

Spencer Tracy, Robert Ryan
1955

Bad Day at Black Rock is a different kind of movie—intense in its bareness and unembellished story line. To put its plot in a nutshell: A disabled stranger visits the small town of Black Rock, Arizona in the immediate aftermath of World War II. He's there to bestow to a local Japanese farmer a posthumous military medal awarded to his son. But, as it turns out, the town has an appalling secret—a certain past that it does not want unearthed. *Bad Day at Black Rock* is immensely gripping and, in the final analysis, an inspirational narrative intertwined with ample doses of both the good and bad of humanity.

16. *Cocoon*

Brian Dennehy, Wilford Brimley,
Maureen Stapleton, Don Ameche
1985

This is a moving, uplifting, and entertaining movie that combines an alien encounter—a friendly one—with the enduring human desire to discover the fountain of youth. *Cocoon* focuses its lenses on a group of seniors residing in a retirement village who are mysteriously energized with the vitality of their elapsed youth. For the rest of the story, you'll just have to watch the movie.

17. The Shootist

John Wayne, Lauren Bacall, Ron Howard
1976

The Shootist is considered by many to be the legendary John Wayne's best movie. It's also his last. And what makes it so special is that Wayne's character, John Bernard Books, is dying of cancer in the storyline, which the actor was also battling at the time. Essentially, the plot finds a terminally ill gunfighter seeking a place to die quietly and with as much dignity as possible. Let's just say that it doesn't quite work out as Mr. Books would have liked. As you might imagine, the movie's got its fair share of old west–style violence, but it's a remarkable—and, in the final scene, truly inspirational—story of a fierce life lived and the ultimate equalizer, death, which will visit us all eventually.

18. The Best Years of Our Lives

Fredric March, Myrna Loy
1946

This movie from yesteryear tells the stories of three World War II veterans from very different social strata returning home after their overseas service. *The Best Years of Our Lives* is all about readjusting to a brand new world and, in essence, starting over. With plenty of crises to go around here, this classic film runs the gamut of human emotions.

19. About Schmidt

Jack Nicholson, Kathy Bates
2002

When Warren Schmidt unexpectedly loses his wife, he takes to the highways and byways on a mission of self-discovery—and to stop his only daughter from marrying a nincompoop. A rare blend in a movie: funny, thought-provoking, and poignant.

20. *Scrooge*

Albert Finney
1970

Scrooge is a delightful musical adaptation of Charles Dickens's classic Christmas story. Inspirational and entertaining from start to finish, this largely undiscovered gem of a movie is one of the greatest holiday flicks ever produced. You've never seen Ebenezer Scrooge's tale of redemption told until you've seen this version.

Twenty Books that Will Make You Think

When I get a little money, I buy books;
and, if any is left, I buy food and clothes.

—Desiderius Erasmus

You've been importuned on more than one occasion in this book to read books. It's the cheapest and most effective way to stimulate your brain. In fact, this mental workout assumes a higher meaning during your jobless stint, when it would be very easy to fall into a rut and never extricate yourself from it.

The bottom line is that you can ill afford to flounder around in the dumps for very long. The diverse list of books to follow has been crafted, above all else, with *thinking* in mind. It is a blend of nonfiction and fiction—something for everybody's tastes. A thought-provoking thread binds this mini-library together.

Unemployment Benefit #31

You can finally read a book in the comforts of home without the unnecessary and persistent interruptions of reading in the workplace.

1. *Cure for the Common Life: Living in Your Sweet Spot*

Max Lucado

In this book, best-selling author Max Lucado assists you in locating what he deems your "sweet spot" job. The title features a "Sweet Spot Discovery Guide" among its bountiful food for thought.

2. *The Secret*

Rhonda Byrne

New Age self-help author Rhonda Byrne makes the compelling case that your positive thoughts serve as potent magnets that attract the very things you desire, such as health, wealth, and, of course, genuine contentment with your lot in life.

3. *A Brief History of Time*

Stephen Hawking

Gifted theoretical physicist Stephen Hawking furnishes you with a book that nobly attempts to explain—from a scientific perspective—where the universe came from and where it's likely headed in the future.

Hawking accomplishes this not inconsiderable mission with minimal technical jargon and a heaping plateful of conclusions to chew on.

4. *The Last Lecture*

Randy Pausch and Jeffrey Zaslow

When a computer science professor at Carnegie Mellon University participates in the school's Last Lecture series, his presentation stands apart from the pack of pedagogues. It seems that the purpose of the series was to ask myriad professors to deliver a lecture from the perspective that it would be their very last. In other words, what would they want to convey to their students one last time—a précis, as it were, of the sum and substance of what they've uncovered on life's long and winding roads? Well, the forty-six-year-old Professor Pausch delivered his last lecture with terminal pancreatic cancer and an imminent death sentence hanging over his head. *The Last Lecture* is a text version of his inspiring life finish. If you want to view Randy Pausch's in-person lecture, it is available on YouTube.

5. *Team of Rivals: The Political Genius of Abraham Lincoln*

Doris Kearns Goodwin

In this book, historian Doris Kearns Goodwin reveals once again the true greatness of Abraham Lincoln. Goodwin, however, adds new depth to Lincoln, documenting the man's unreserved willingness to appoint a cabinet teeming with past nemeses and very ambitious rivals. Lincoln wanted what was best for the country in perilous times and put any ego concerns of his own on hold. What's most compelling about this fascinating read are the many remarkable correspondences included in the text. People communicated in handwritten letters back in the day before the telephone, e-mail, and text messaging. And, you know what? The men and women from the nineteenth century seemed perfectly capable of expressing heartfelt feelings. They did it, too, quite eloquently and sans the help of Dr. Phil.

6. *The Last Lion: Alone (1932–1940)*

William Manchester

This book is historian and biographer William Manchester's second installment on the fascinating life of Winston Churchill. Manchester never got around to penning the final installment of Churchill's last years. Nevertheless, this particular edition chronicles Churchill's words and actions in the years leading up to World War II. You see the man, as the subtitle indicates, standing alone in warning about the impending dangers and dark cloud spreading over Europe and, indeed, the world. Churchill's clarion call is eternal.

7. *Shakespeare: The Invention of the Human*

Harold Bloom

In this book, controversial literary critic Harold Bloom writes, "The ultimate use of Shakespeare is to let him teach you to think too well, to whatever truth you can sustain without perishing." Bloom feels that "no one" has "yet managed to be post-Shakespeare." He views the Bard as the greatest literary intellect of all time and makes a compelling case for just that in *Shakespeare: The Invention of the Human*.

8. *The Death of Ivan Ilyich*

Leo Tolstoy

This novella, initially published in 1886, is rightly considered a classic of Russian literature. There's a whole lot of food for thought packed into this short book. Highly readable more than a century later (in its English translation no less), *The Death of Ivan Ilyich* will not only engage you with a good read, but it'll get you thinking on such weighty matters as suffering, illness, and the meaning of life.

9. *Catcher in the Rye*

J. D. Salinger

When a novel stands the test of time like J. D. Salinger's *Catcher in the Rye*, it pays to pick it up and find out what all the fuss is about. First published in 1951, many of us had to read this book in high school. Why not try reading it now from your more adult perspective? It's astounding that Holden Caulfield remains an icon for rebellious teens after all those years. Written in the first person from Mr. Caulfield's unique perspective, the novel is still controversial more than a half century later. Courtesy of its generous sprinkling of profanity, teen angst, and sexuality, it's sure to entertain and engage you in your adult mind and body.

10. *Ladies of Liberty: The Women Who Shaped Our Nation*

Cokie Roberts

In *Ladies of Liberty*, veteran ABC news reporter and anchor Cokie Roberts recounts the history of our nation's founding from the atypical perspective of our founding mothers. This title definitely adds a necessary—but often overlooked—layer to the history books.

11. *Autobiography of a Yogi*

Paramahansa Yogananda

No, this isn't a book by the philosopher Yogi Berra. It's a different yogi here. This autobiography has been translated into twenty languages. It addresses questions on subject matter ranging from religion to God to life's ultimate purpose to yoga to higher consciousness. That's quite a mouthful. If you're looking to decipher the true meaning of life, this Yogi could be of some help. If he turns out not to be, there's always Yogi Berra, who has some pretty sensible views on things, too.

12. *The Iceman Cometh*

Eugene O'Neill

This title is a tragedy in four acts. *The Iceman Cometh* is a play completed in 1939 that revolves around a cadre of alcoholic oddballs who incessantly talk about their hopes and dreams but, alas, never fulfill them. There are definitely lessons to be learned here.

13. *A Nation of Sheep*

Andrew P. Napolitano

Judge Andrew Napolitano is a familiar face on television these days, perpetually commenting on the legal matters—both small and large—of our time. The judge is also an unstinting champion of our fundamental liberties. *A Nation of Sheep* makes the case that the federal government is continually circumventing the Constitution, and slowly but surely gnawing away at our basic rights as American citizens, which are the underpinnings of our democracy. It's worth hearing what the judge has to say. You can be the judge, then, whether or not you feel his arguments are solid.

14. *Travels with Charley: In Search of America*

John Steinbeck

In 1960, renowned American novelist John Steinbeck took to the highways and byways of America with his French standard poodle, Charley, and no other living creature. After the novelist's death in 1968, Steinbeck's son revealed that the ailing author knew he wasn't long for this earth and wanted to experience one last hurrah in the wider world. *Travels with Charley* is an intriguing travelogue from start to finish. Interestingly, unlike his popular novels—*The Grapes of Wrath, Of Mice and Men*, and *The Winter of Our Discontent*—this book never landed on any school reading lists. Now is your opportunity to read a Steinbeck title that your high-school English classes didn't require.

15. *The Kin of Ata Are Waiting for You*

Dorothy Bryant

If you are you interested in taking a symbolic voyage of the soul, as it were, then *The Kin of Ata Are Waiting for You* is waiting for you. This rather obscure title imparts the tale of a deeply distressed man running away from fast times, fame, fortune, drug use, and crime. But when this lost soul meets the kin of Ata, things really get cooking. If nothing else, this book will get you thinking.

16. *The Prince*

Niccolo Machiavelli

When a book published in 1513 maintains its relevance these many centuries later, it's worth checking out. The author has even spawned a word we're familiar with: Machiavellian. *The Prince* is, in fact, a political treatise that addresses relevant political and moral issues that still resonate in the twenty-first century.

17. *Moby-Dick*

Herman Melville

This novel debuted in 1851 and recounts the story of a sailor named Ishmael on a dangerous and gritty whaling ship voyage onto the high seas. *Moby-Dick* delves into the universal and timeless themes of good versus evil on numerous levels via the interaction of characters. It's anything but a big fish story.

18. *The Nat Hentoff Reader*

Nat Hentoff

This intriguing book is a compendium of the writings of iconoclast and genuine civil libertarian Nat Hentoff. Hentoff has been a tireless defender of the First Amendment and has waged battle with all sides of the political spectrum. In an age of increasing political partisanship and inane political correctness, Hentoff shines as man of genuine principle, whether you agree with him or not.

19. *The Jungle*

Upton Sinclair

Published in 1906, *The Jungle* is a fictional accounting of the nonfictional corruption in Chicago's meatpacking industry at the turn of the twentieth century. Employing the character of Jurgis Rudkus, a Lithuanian immigrant, to tell a gripping story, Sinclair's novel is widely credited with spawning a revolution against the kind of exploitation and abuse that was rampant in that bygone era. *The Jungle* is a gripping read as a piece of literature and food for thought on top of that. In fact, you might think twice before putting a hamburger or pork chop in your mouth after reading this novel.

20. *Father Joe*

Tony Hendra

This is comedy writer Tony Hendra's memoir, but it's not about editing *National Lampoon* magazine or putting funny dialogue into the mouths of Chevy Chase and John Belushi. Rather, it's the recounting of his unique spiritual journey aided and abetted by a self-effacing Benedictine monk named Father Joseph Warrillow.

PART FOUR

FEELING GOOD

Finding Support Among Family and Friends

Call it a clan, call it a network, call it a tribe, call it a family.
Whatever you call it, whoever you are, you need one.

—Jane Howard

W hen unemployment knocks on your door, your existing family life cannot help but be simultaneously disrupted. There's no getting around it; the people in your inner sanctum are impacted in countless ways by your joblessness. This is not an opportune time to hunker down in a self-imposed physical and emotional bunker. It's in your best interests to tell both close family members and tried-and-true friends the ABCs of your current jobless situation, including your immediate plans for the future.

Interaction with Close Family and Friends

Generally speaking, it's best to tell the whole truth, and nothing but the truth, to those closest to you. Little is gained by fudging the facts, or by painting a picture of your circumstances that doesn't quite mesh with reality. Be upfront with your family and friends, and:

✦ Let them know precisely what you need from them at this seminal moment in your life—*and what you don't need!*

✦ Express your genuine feelings. If you want to cry—let the tears flow. If you feel like laughing, don't let anybody make you feel guilty about it.

✦ Establish—in a nice way—definitive boundaries. In other words, let those closest to you know what your jobless days and nights will look like—i.e., when you want to be left alone in both your job pursuits *and* leisure activities.

Emotional Support ABCs

In the big picture, unemployment can be a very rocky road with its fair share of potholes along the way. So, it's obviously preferable to have a few compatible copilots in your life, if you will, who are not backseat drivers. That is, you need empathetic and unstinting emotional support from those in your tight-knit circle. This doesn't mean your family has to engage in a group hug every single day while you're out of work. Rather, the brand of emotional support we are talking about should be:

✦ **Non-judgmental.** Essentially, you don't want the people in your life critiquing every action *and inaction* of your joblessness—telling you, for instance, where to look for a job. Nor do you need to hear perpetual carping about your job search methodologies. In the final analysis, people saying that you're not doing enough to find work, not looking in the right places, and having way too much fun is not going to help.

- ✦ **Available.** It's good to have one or more close family members and friends who are the proverbial phone call away—folks at the ready to hear you out (non-judgmentally, of course).

- ✦ **Unobtrusive.** On the other side of the emotional support fence are wide-open spaces. Bona fide emotional support knows when to say when. Really, you can't abide family and friends hovering around you like a flock of vultures eyeing a carcass-in-waiting.

The Family Foundation

Yes, at the foundation of your social network are, naturally, members of your family—your kith and kin. For most of us, the family unit remains at the epicenter of our lives from first burps to last gasps. Fundamentally, family—no matter its rating on the dysfunctional scale—will be there for you, come what may, for all the times of your life. This isn't to suggest that all families—or even most of them, for that matter—offer the requisite emotional support and sufficient succor commensurate with life's unpredictable roller-coaster ride. However, more times than not, families are—at the very least—consistent physical presences in our lives when what we need, foremost, are familiar faces.

Let us assume that you need a small loan to tide you over until you land a paying job. Who is the very first person you'd consider putting the bite on? Your ex-boss? Highly unlikely! Your good friend and former colleague at the office? Possibly. Your lifelong buddy from your childhood days? More likely. But how about your parents or a sibling? This familial route is more often than not the pathway of least resistance in this dicey area. We are more apt to humble ourselves at the feet of the folks who know us best and for the longest amounts of time. And, if you want to add a little more meat to this food for thought about asking for a loan, chew on this one: If your unemployment days and nights drag on longer than you bargain for, and you can no longer afford to pay your rent or mortgage, who would you temporarily move in with? Would it be a member of your family or a non-relative? For most of us, the answer would be the former.

Friends

The next layer of your network should be liberally sprinkled with your friends. The old saying, "You can choose your friends, but not your relatives," no doubt resonates with a lot of people. The friends you make in life—who are part of your social network—are in your orbit because of certain shared values, interests, and experiences.

When you're out of a job and on the prowl for another line of work, your friends often assume the role of kingmakers in ensuring that it's a smooth transition. Even if they aren't involved in actually supplying you with a hot job tip, your friends are vital conduits to keeping you active, positive, and forward-moving during your period of unemployment.

A healthy serving of the suggestions in this book—notably those revolving around having some fun, beating back stress, relaxing, and remaining social—ask that you partner with your fellow human beings. That is, go places and do things with your fellow man and fellow woman. Most often these pairings will be with members of your family or good friends.

It Takes Two to Tango

When you're out of job, plug into your network with unrestrained abandon. Yes, to help you locate the right kind of work, but also to remain upbeat and on an even emotional keel. Get together with family and friends and *do*—period. While many of these suggestions have been mentioned in one fashion or another in earlier parts of this book, here is a short list of possible things you can do with family and friends:

+ Take long walks
+ Go out for a jog
+ Go hiking
+ Go camping
+ Walk your dogs together
+ Join a library book club together
+ Take a crafting class
+ Take a painting class
+ Attend community meetings
+ Participate in a community project
+ Join a fitness club together
+ Go out to breakfast, lunch, or dinner
+ Organize a yard or house sale together
+ Share a table at a flea market
+ Go to the movies

And this list could go on and on. Whatever depth of support exists in your unique network, it behooves you to excavate it for all it's worth *now*, when you are a jobless soul, but also in the future, when you are on the top of the world again.

With Whom Should You Get in Touch?

Friends and acquaintances are the surest passport to fortune.

—Arthur Schopenhauer

Beyond the solid underpinning of your network—family and friends—there's a vast ocean out there for you to cast your net. In your current incarnation as a jobless statistic, it's always a prudent policy to reach out and touch someone, and another someone, and another someone after that. Expand your contacts until your address book spits the names back at you.

There are, in fact, countless areas to forage for worthwhile contacts. Look upon the building of your network as both an employment and social safety net. In other words, the more people you know—in a variety of capacities—the less likely it is that you'll end up on skid row.

EXERCISE
Choosing Your Contacts

So, just who should you consider getting in touch with to lubricate your transition from joblessness to the very best possible job, career, or new business? By asking yourself a flurry of related questions, you'll acquire a good handle on exactly who is pledge caliber for your network fraternity. Here's a fair sampling of the kinds of questions both to ask and to answer as you establish an ocean full of contacts.

1. With whom do I feel most at ease speaking on an intimate basis?

   _____

2. With whom do I most enjoy getting together for social events and daily activities?

   _____

3. Are there people I've previously worked alongside who are presently employed in areas of interest to me?

   _____

4. Is there a family member, or friend of mine, who knows somebody who could assist me in landing a good job?

   _____

5. Are there any neighbors of mine with whom I'd like to connect on a personal level? A business level?

   _____

6. Are there persons from my past with whom I've lost touch that would complement my current network?

   _____

7. Are there members of my local community with whom I could make contact for possible employment leads?

   _____

8. Are there any individuals from my last job—or previous jobs before that—who could help me in my present job search?

   _____

9. Who among the acquaintances encountered in my everyday activities can supply me with potential job and career leads?

   _____

10. Are there any persons from my various alma maters—college, high school, and grade school—who could aid me in procuring future employment?

   _____

11. Who among my friends can help me take my mind *off* of things like job searches and finances?

   _____

Branching Out: Finding Friends in New Places

The one thing in the world, of value, is the active soul.

—Ralph Waldo Emerson

We've heretofore addressed the subject of networking from the somewhat narrow perspective of people you know or knew. That is, building your network with the life hand you've thus far been dealt. But, come on now, you've also got a golden opportunity to play those life cards by simply experiencing *new* things and visiting *new* places. By boldly going where you've never before trod, you meet new people—men and women who, in some instances, could become key players on your network team.

What follows is a roster of twenty ideas to assist you in accomplishing the aforementioned mission of charting new territory. Some of the possibilities are very specific, while others are broad concepts, enabling you to plug in the unique particulars of your personality and life circumstances. Consider this the all-important Phase II in your network-building game.

1. Everybody Lives in a Community, Including You

There's no getting around the fact that you live in a community of individuals. So, right off the bat, you've got something in common with either a whole mess of people or, if you call home a rural hamlet, a somewhat smaller demographic. Whatever their exact census numbers, neighbors can assume significant roles in your growing network.

Explore the chief concerns facing your community and attend any local meetings that occur. Volunteer your time vis-à-vis community matters. If you require assistance in this networking terrain, you might just find MeetTheNeighbors.com helpful. This website brings neighbors together and empowers them with the tips, tools, and techniques to communicate, organize, and—of course—socialize.

2. The Jaycees

The United States Junior Chamber of Commerce (Jaycees) at USJaycees.org is an organization that could very possibly augment your network of contacts. The only fly in the ointment is that this outfit is for young folks only. If you're past the decrepit age of forty-one, you'll have to look elsewhere for a networking boost.

If you meet the age requirements, the Jaycees could definitely assist you in locating a job, career, or business startup. It's a group that will, at the very least, facilitate meetings with new people, furnish potential job leads, and supply timely information on what's happening in your community with regards to the *business* at hand.

3. YMCA and YWCA

These two organizations—one for men, YMCA.net, and one for women, YWCA.org—are, above all else, committed to enhancing youngsters' lives, building stronger families, and improving communities by encouraging volunteerism. Many neighborhoods throughout the country are fortunate enough to have YMCA and YWCA centers—with their trademark fitness programs (including swimming pools)—on their terra firma. In the big picture, YMCA and YWCA outfits are essentially places to lend a helping hand while meeting fellow helpers and helpees.

4. Alumni Associations

If you are a graduate from a college or university, you are an alumnus. There is also an alumni association waiting with open arms for you and, yes, a pecuniary contribution of some sort. Alumni groups regularly organize social events and encourage networking. They publish newsletters which detail the adventures of their membership.

Don't forget, too, that high schools also have alumni associations. Fear not descending the ladder a few rungs. You're all adults now. In addition, if you were a member of a fraternity or sorority in your college days, these esteemed outfits haven't forgotten you. Once you're an accepted pledge, you're a pledge for life. It's sort of like a tattoo. So, by all means, take advantage of this permanent brand in your networking odyssey.

5. Digg This

The website Digg.com proclaims that it is all about "Sharing and Discovery." It is a cyber spot for news, videos, images, and podcasts that are submitted entirely by the Digg community, which consists of humble sorts just like you. Get yourself out there any way you can. That's how networks become NETWORKS.

6. One Picture Is Worth a Thousand Words

If you've got photographs that you want accessible to your current network—family, friends, and others—in one fell swoop, showcase them on Flickr.com. This website portal decrees, "Share Your Photos, Watch the World." In other words, there are a lot of folks who are members of Flickr, and some of them just might be interested in your images. Remember the old saying: Seeing is believing.

7. Share and Share Alike

Since we're on the subject of networking beyond the traditional comfort zone, you might consider joining an online community with a mission to bring people together with shared interests. In fact, it's a community that facilitates business connections and romantic connections, too. And, by the way, there are no laws that prohibit seeking both at the same time. So, check out Orkut.com and bolster your network with, for starters, virtual contact and then—who knows?—physical contact.

8. Political Activism

No matter where you land on the political spectrum, there are opportunities for networking therein. Conservative, liberal, Republican, Democrat—it doesn't matter. You could join a local political party organization.

You could also get involved with issue-oriented groups, be they supporting abortion rights or gun rights or anything in between. In other words, translate your political leanings into network building. For assistance in this fertile area, visit SpeakOut.com, which is a website chock-full of information on both the issues of the day and the pathways to activism. In fact, the site features copious links to advocacy groups that run the entire left-to-right gamut.

9. Save the Planet

There are an awful lot of people all across the world who prefer not to swim in waste waters and breathe Los Angeles–style smog. If environmental issues mean something to you, there are environmental groups aplenty that would be as pleased as punch to welcome you as a member. Check out ActionNetwork.org, which will furnish you with the names and websites of the leading environmental advocacy organizations. There are excellent networking possibilities here, as there are in just about all outfits dedicated to a cause.

10. Rotary Clubs

The motto of Rotary International is "Service Above Self." And you've probably spotted local Rotary Club signs along many highways and byways in your travels. Did you ever wonder what on earth a Rotary Club is, and who its members are?

Well, Rotary International is the world's pioneering service club. Its individual chapters consist of volunteers. Visit Rotary.org for further information on Rotary Clubs and what they do. Many Rotarians are well-connected members of their respective communities, which should be of interest to you.

11. Business Networking

If you want to sample a networking outfit that is specifically dedicated to business, look no further than Ryze.com. Members can erect network-oriented homepages to attract *quality* business contacts.

12. You Can Never Have Too Many of Them

True friends are rare and hard to come by. So, it behooves you to perpetually be chumming for buddies. FriendFinder.com allows you to run personal ads for whatever your heart desires, including a good time and a little loving.

13. Blog Away

It's the twenty-first century. So, if you want to build your network by reaching out to new folks, a blog of your own could be just what the doctor ordered. But it's not going to do you any good to blog away, and blog away some more, and—in the end—reach the virtual audience equivalent of a black hole.

To extend your network, why not seek to fashion your own blog network, if you will? For a better understanding how this voluble cyber bailiwick functions, call on HomeTurfMedia.com and 9Rules.com. Reach as many people as you can with your blogging insight. It's a network builder for sure.

14. The Right Links

At LinkedIn.com, you will encounter a website business with the mission to strengthen and build your existing network. And since that's precisely what this entire section is all about, why not have a look-see?

15. Best Friends on Four Legs

The pet care industry is growing in leaps and bounds because of the incredible bond that people feel for their companion animals. Pets are now unmistakable members of the family and we are "pet parents." This sociological phenomenon has introduced a variety of networking possibilities.

In other words, employ your love of animals to meet fellow animal lovers. Volunteer at an animal shelter. Join a club devoted to your specific breed of cat or dog. Gather and frolic with fellow canine parents and their canines at park runs. Join organizations, such as the Humane Society of the United States at HSUS.org.

16. Make Networking Your Hobby

Whatever you call your hobbies or special interests, there are like-minded folks out there who share them. These are prime possibilities for your budding network. Many hobbies have clubs and societies for their devotees' benefit. Attend events and shows in your hobby field. Talk and trade with your fellow hobbyists.

17. Convert Your Talents Into a Network

Whether you have a knack for crafting or painting; whether you can fix cars or computers; whether you can tickle the ivories on a piano or strum the strings on a guitar, there are networking opportunities amidst one and all of these special talents and countless others, too.

Just place yourself on life's big stage, even if it's in your little sliver of the world. Let people see and experience your extraordinary genius. Artistic? You could attend arts and crafts shows and sell your creations. Handy? You could volunteer your services as Mr. Fix It at a senior citizen center and elsewhere. A musical talent? Play the piano at a local watering hole or a church function.

18. Network Channeling

In a previous chapter, we noted that posting videos on YouTube.com was an interesting avenue to travel down for a whole host of reasons. And you don't have to post home videos of yourself and your friends pulling people's pants down or anything like that. You can post less personal productions, such as clips from television programs or movies. Once you put videos up for the entire world to see, people slowly but surely visit your channel, as it's called, and could eventually become your *subscribers* and *friends*. As you can appreciate, there are potential networking tentacles in all of this.

19. Start a Group

This is the Information Age. Hence, you have opportunities galore to initiate cyber groups. In fact, you could host your own group today on Groups.Yahoo.com or Groups.MSN.com. There are discussion groups devoted to every imaginable subject and interest.

Why not establish a group dedicated to the travails of unemployment, inviting members to share ideas on how to best weather the storm, as well as their personal experiences? You'd be surprised how many people would sign on to your group, and some of these folks could become integral parts of your growing network.

20. Instant Networking

We would be remiss if we did not reiterate the names of the two most popular social networking websites on the Internet: MySpace.com and

Facebook.com. These two cyber portals are rooted in meeting people with common interests. They enable their members both to promote themselves and to connect with the wider world.

One final word as it relates to these two virtual meeting spots and, for that matter, all others: It behooves you to be constantly vigilant in keeping your eyes and ears open for potential bullies and predators. By practicing the fine art of common sense at all times, you'll realize the full benefits of these virtual networking possibilities without ever getting bruised and blistered along the way.

Just Say No: No Job? No Prob!

*When more and more people
are thrown out of work, unemployment results.*

—President Calvin Coolidge

O kay, now that you've read and digested every single morsel of this book, you obviously know the score: No job? No prob! Honestly, what in tarnation is the point in raising your blood pressure over the loss of a job? Why suffer through another restless night? Is there any good that can come out of blowing a mental gasket at this important crossroads in your life? No, there's nothing at all gained by worrying around the clock and decrying your lot as a member of the unemployment fraternity!

The various chapters of this book underscore time and again the significance of being both proactive and upbeat during your joblessness. Proactive, of course, in conscientiously pursuing your next rewarding job, career, or business undertaking. But vigilantly upbeat, too, in

299

wading through your unemployment days and nights with both a smile and positive attitude. The sum and substance of this book is not—by any stretch of the imagination—meant to diminish the consequences of job loss. Nor is it intended to make light of its potentially weighty ramifications. On the contrary, *No Job? No Prob!* is, first and foremost, a celebration of human resilience. That is, your capacity to rise from the jobless ashes wiser and more durable than ever before.

If all went as planned, plowing through the pages of *No Job? No Prob!* opened a bay-sized window for you—one that allowed a fresh and cleansing breeze to blow through your wobbly psyche. Indeed, if you follow this book's leads, you will emerge—for sure—more refreshed, clearer-headed, and smarter for the next chapter and verse in your life story. And—here's the ultimate kicker—you'll have a heaping helping of fun and good times, too! Look upon *No Job? No Prob!* as both an informative and entertaining blueprint that shows you how to solidly connect with one of life's sharpest curveballs—unemployment—and hit a few home runs along the way. Keep it handy and refer to it whenever you need a lift or idea.

Yes, you've experienced an abrupt ending with the loss of your job. But you didn't land on a dead-end street. In fact, you are primed at the starting gate once again. Rev your engines. Ready . . . set . . . GO!